The Weight of Addition

an anthology of Texas Poetry

edited by Randall Watson

Mutabilis Press
Houston

Published by:

Mutabilis Press
3514 Deal St.
Houston, Texas 77025
www.mutabilispress.org

Printed in the United States of America

Library of Congress Control Number: 2007938160
ISBN 978-0-9729432-3-9

THE WEIGHT OF ADDITION

FOREWORD

With each book, our purpose at Mutabilis Press—to serve our community of poets by offering them a place where their work is thoughtfully considered for publication—becomes clearer. In addition to serving both the well and under published, our goal is to integrate the work of critically recognized poets with those who are seriously writing poems, but not directly connected with, or currently in, an academic program. I know, and once again feel passionately, that this inclusiveness can only create more lovers of poetry, expanding every poet's sense of what poetry is and can be.

In *The Weight of Addition, an anthology of Texas Poetry,* Randall Watson brings together the diverse work of many fine poets living in Texas. There are several poets who no longer live here, but they are included because of their lasting influence on many poets and readers who do.

As with any collaborative effort there are many faithful and hard working individuals who have helped make this book possible. Without the enthusiasm and knowledge of our guest editor, Randall Watson, this book would not have had the richness and dimension that it does. Through the entire process, although challenging at times, we never felt a loss of faith in the project. Randy was a pleasure to work with, taking everything in stride. He offered his ideas freely to us, who are still learning much about poetry and publishing. We are grateful to him for this.

I wish to thank the enduring board of Mutabilis Press: Joe Barnes, Kristi Beer, Stan Crawford, Gretchen Jameson, Jano Nixon, and Iris Rozencwajg, for their confidence, hard work and friendship. Much gratitude goes to cover artist Frank White, for his imagination and generosity. Thanks also to Janice Martin for her willingness to copy edit a poetry book, and to Varsha Shah, for her encouragement and help with reading. And finally, I give unending thanks to my life collaborator, Bob, and his sidekicks—our children, Daniel and Julia—who ground me in the real world.

Carolyn Tourney Florek
Managing Editor / Publisher

TABLE OF CONTENTS

INTRODUCTION

Texas has always been a land of continual and repetitive migrations. Neither simply the culture of the traditional south, of the heartland nor old west, of its indigenous peoples nor of Spain, of Mexico nor the U.S., it is nonetheless each of these, and all of them, and none. It is both the gulf—that gap between things—that receives the rivers, and the rivers themselves.

To see it as such, I believe, constitutes a kind of civic good, as far as one agrees that to acknowledge a complex reality is preferable to taking refuge in the simplicity and comfort of a distortion.

So the reader of this collection won't find much to reify that old story about ranches and haciendas and oil, of tin roofs and bead-board, armadillos and long-horned cattle, though their absence isn't a criticism. In part an effect of the proliferation of Creative Writing Programs and the influence they have on local culture, this is also the result of a populace that is increasingly diverse, not just anglo and chicano, but Indian and Japanese, Polish and Lebanese. In the most basic sense, it is the sign of a statewide care for poetry and an embracing of the values inherent within it: of attention, of consideration and feeling; of examination; of the kind of honesty that rejects the sentimental and easy ordering of the world; of the rush and joy of language.

It is my intention, then, that the title, *The Weight of Addition*, should suggest the depth and range of the work that appears here. For each of these poems—about life on the land, about crawdads and windmills and rivers, about Rabbis and drag queens and internment camps—each is an addition—increasingly multinational, multi-sensational—of language, culture, sensibility, idiom. Each is an accumulation of blessing or of loss—an enlargement, the way joy enlarges us, or grief—

15

multiple, various, diverse—a sum—and how we are magnified by it, strengthened or broken. Each transforms us, potentially, in its expansiveness, through what is held up and offered.

And thus each naturally possesses a kind of weight as well—a kind of gravity and seriousness, a presence—substantial and individual—that seeks its acknowledgement—like the unavoidable intransigencies of memory or fact—both their call and burden—something that must be turned to and met—like a stranger at the door. In this, the accumulations of temperament and habit and blood, the assumptions and secrecies; in this, the weight of otherness and the distances from which it arises; in this, the heaviness that too often comes between and upon us, yet resolves, eventually, hopefully, into a kind of ballast, which, running the full length of the hold, can give a ship at sea its stability and center.

This is the poet's work: to bear experience; to hold it, lift it, make of it a gesture and a world, a surface and witness; to make audible our labor and what labors within us: the perpetual arrivals, accretions, small and large—an inheritance transformed and welcomed, a legacy built on and saved. Even abandoned.

This, I hope, is what the reader will find here. An anthology is a kind of community, a network of additions. And poetry is a counter weight to isolation, a span which links the solitude of one person to the solitude of another, and is thus transcendent in its impulse and function—and ultimately, a form of generosity.

And so—we have the poems themselves: each a sign and a revelation of our uncommon lives and their incorporations: each an artifact of the spirit, of the inner life with its mass and fluidity, its knowledge of relation and loss: each an addition and a weight—humane and troubled and hopeful and necessary—a mirror in which we might discover not just those things that distinguish us, but those that identify us, that connect us, individually, in what might be called our mutuality, our belonging.

Randall Watson

Editor's Choice Awards

First Place:

D. B. Cherry, Diptych

Second Place:

Monica Teresa Ortiz, Dentist Appointment

Third Place:

Kate Schmitt, Afterworld

Honorable Mentions:

Larry L. Fontenot, Mowing Deconstructed
Melanie Jordan, Liminal

THE WEIGHT OF ADDITION

V. T. Abercrombie

AFTER THE RAIN,

the pond poses as if to please
a landscape artist. Even a heron,
legs in the shallows, quiet, listens
to the minnow's thin song,
contemplates dinner. Inside,
the dead rat in the wall no longer
smells, plays host to a fly hatch

that descends from the air conditioning
vent, surrounds me like a host
of night thoughts, like the air flow
and hum of the doctor's words,
mastectomy metastic carcinoma,
four centimeters. When my tongue
grows ulcers from the chemo—

good cells die, bad cells grow—
I think about cycles: scum on the pond,
fish in the heron's belly, the nurturing
rat, fast growing cancer cells, lost
hair, tongue health and I know
I can't step out of this landscape,
or hide from life's unfettered feast.

Carolyn Adams

TESTAMENT

Within a stand of tall cedars,
a doe fell prey in early spring,

her panicked eye reflecting white
from a predatory moon.

The ground shifted beneath her feet,
then settled back to what it was,

her falling body fitted to
the hollows of the wooded field.

She lies there still, her tattered pelt
now emptied by the scavengers

who kept their watch and cleaned each bone
of all its necessary flesh.

As the southern constellations
sweep light and dust in equal measure,

the grass sings in a testament
to what the turning earth provides.

The night birds leave their nesting trees
to fold into the winter dark,

and take their places in the sky
against another hungry moon.

THE LONG DEFEAT

Muriel's wasted for
sixteen years.
No one notices.
She sleeps,
standing.

Generations of swans
gather in stairwells
filled with water,
with wine.
A flower in a
cave behind a gate
blooms all day,
all day.

She is sick
from the scent of
that vigilant flower.
She has fallen
into silence.
She has been struck
nameless.

Though she's shelved
bone-to-bone,
Muriel throws her
arms deep into a dream-song,
pulling out
a man, a woman,
dark trees,
a bright sun.

She waits to tell this:
One need
will turn the flower
to a flame.

James Adams

BEGINNING WITH DOOM IN A BULB

> *"Beginning with doom in the bulb,*
>   *the spring unravels ..."*
> —*Dylan Thomas, "I, In My Intricate Image"*

Beginning with doom in a bulb,
        the bright light turns to spring
upon the dark of day's end—

for with this intricate image
        we, two, begin
a length of string which numbers our day.

What ray do we then send?
        to twist the knob electric upon
its blown glass and tungsten-drawn place—

pick the quick of this filamented cryst,
shutter this, our midnight tryst:

for with this intricate image
        we, too, end.

Alan Ainsworth

A SERMON IN THE WOODS

The genius of the situation is this:
hogs, wild, hunters with rusted guns,
a pitfall filled in—

Late fall, and I feel lawless,
without form, past forms
struggled past

"Adopt these ways . . ."
   flashes—
          shots fired—
          before us—
Behind nothing.
     ". . . these ways"

Envy the dead, envy the living.
Some are everywhere,
Ragged, surprised, stunned.

BARELY TURNED

Barely turned, him three-quarters
    away
        and we take measures
    to keep it that way—

Against meaning, against metaphor.
Against the moment. The moment.

Making faces, funny ones,
    sticking out tongues—
losing tempers, quarreling,
    nothing but irritation.

Now tickling, now cussing.

Not anything but lousy.

Who isn't nervous about what is to come . . . ?

I know we're never reckless
    No—
        Sharp, maybe, a thorn

some want greener, or never.
    Some want sudden, some not.

Needle a thread, thread a needle,
whole cloth made into sail.
attach, look,

gone.

Mike Alexander

CHARYBDIS

I brought the white clothes—lambs-wool sacrifice,
our cotton mesh, our lost warmth, sweat-stained,
the reptilian skins we shucked off to replace

in secret, venom-streaked, but rattle-brained
secretions in the grass, a tire's screech,
convulsions. Working in the basement, chained,

beside a tool bench, badly-stocked, out of reach,
before a storage bin below the stairs—
I opened up the Whirlpool, added bleach

& liquid Tide to gym socks, folded pairs,
a change of sheets, extra-large undershirt
& underwear. In antiseptic chores,

our nightmares rally strength. Like week-old dirt,
our whites showed the regrets, the faded vows,
perpetual mortgage of a ground-in hurt.

I tried to pass for exemplary spouse,
while feeling like a termite in the wood
gnawing at the foundation of our house,

I felt the mortar wash away for good.
I felt exposed to adder-lidded eyes.
I felt the Whirlpool spinning in my blood.

Barry Ballard

SIX THOUSAND PRAYERS

In another solar system there's an unknown
family burying one of its children,
in a ritual of sky-like halftones
we can only imagine. And the end
of their light, their sorrow, only reaches
us after their grieving has already
taken place, a star of prayers among the speechless
dying six thousand they say we can see

with our naked eye. And even the parents
dead before they could plead with us that their
child deserved a life, already their words
nothing but the soft bleeding dust of red
hydrogen, their fear not even creasing
our rituals of despair, our blue atmosphere.

Alicia Bankston

ASAN MEMORIAL, GUAM

Under glass, the battery and boot-stomp
of Asan beach fades.
In black and white
the first Marine invasion, stickered
with tiny white arrows and Times New Roman font.
Bronze, in bas-relief, 1941.

We, too, glassed that clatter
the munitions, sirens. Sometimes still
you sit up straight in half-sleep
to the scud alert's long screech.
I can see you, back pressed into the cold stone
barricade, gas mask in one hand, smoke lit
in the other. Even the tattoo on your chest—
these colors never run—fades,
in bas-relief, in memoriam.
We keep lights on
to drown out gray shadows,

the same shadows—war etched
into the landscape. The whole island
so black with ash our military
dumped tangan-tangan seeds from B17s
to start it growing.
Now in Piti, beach crabs battle
for a miniature pillbox.
One always skitters away sideways

alone. I cling
like Irish pennants to your shirt.
You, still etched
by Saudi Arabia's dust,
were used to folding your underwear
into tiny squares—the life soldiers
could contain, square inch
by square inch.

At Asan Point, where sand covers
coral bits, it is hard to imagine
a discolored sun. The last shells
are buried in the roots of coconut
and tangan-tangan. The only holes
are crab-holes the size of fists.

Wendy Barker

APOLOGY FOR BLUE

> *"Don't prate to me of divinity ... but of blue."*
> —*William Gass (1924-   )*

A form of black, said the Greeks,
cousin of gray, species
of darkness, opposite of light,
not a mention in Homer
with his wine-dark seas.

Even the Bible doesn't note
the celestial vault is blue.
We've three times more synonyms
for red—cerulean lacks
the force of blood's vermilion.

And yet Cennini's quattrocento
brought back lapis lazuli
from Badakshan, ground
the heavy, gray-veined stone
to paste, kneaded it like bread,

sieved, melted, strained the stuff
through linen, then mixed in lye
and slapped the lump with sticks
till the blue drained off, a powder
stored in a leather purse.

Reserved for the Virgin's lap.
Color of meekness and profound
piety, the heavenly spirit,
that woman's body cool, unsullied
by carnality, wrapped in blue

more dear than gold.
But nineteenth-century scientists
observed, in the Bunsen burner's
flame, the highest heat is blue.
The hottest stars are bluish white,

and objects hurtling near light speed
show bluer than the slower ones —
in physics, blue's the color
of collision, fire, the laser's beam
that centuries of artists showed

streaming to a mortal woman's lap:
fulcrum of our heated lives,
hinge and spring of our renewal.
Hard to see what's closest.
From the moon, earth is blue.

Wendy Barker

COMPOSITION IN GRAY

Dust to dust, not even that, for dirt is yellow, brown, or red.
Ashes, not even that, for these are also chunks of bone.

Desaturated light, the volume turned below our vision.
Her pulse at twelve, then under seven beats a minute.

Throat-choking fog through night and noon, a pall that blurs
angles of walls, the street signs turned to fuzz, illegible.

Our senses can't discern the subtler shades
of avian plumage, the various grays on chickadees.

Not even that. As though her ashes in the jar had drifted out
and, lofted by the air, have sifted over everything.

And now the lake has died, the parasites, giardia, the scum
of algae multiplied, loons abandoning their nests.

Buried within the Munsell Color System's inner core,
achromatic, oxymoron, color of no color.

And still she stares at us from photographs.
A cinema in black and white, continuously reeling.

At the end, I stroked her toes, bare of their familiar polish.
Within the room, not even shadows, even shade.

COSMIC DEBRIS

When I was twelve I was
struck by a meteor.

It wasn't very large,
true, as meteors go —

the size, tops, of a new
pea — but still big enough

to break my shoulder blade
and earn me a story

(page two above the fold)
in our local paper.

The meteor hit me
but I hit the jackpot.

The headline read *BILLION
TO ONE ODDS, EXPERT SAYS.*

I forget the expert's
name but not my nurse's:

Beverly Kramer, she
of the rich starched bosom,

who cooed as she told me
what a brave boy I was.

I fell in fame. I fell
in love. I was special

for a month of awestruck
friends and follow-up trips

to my beloved Bev.
Then, alas, my fracture

healed and a four-year-old
went missing from a park.

I slipped back into my
self. School started, Chloe

had puppies, Mr. Reed
put in a swimming pool,

I learned that some things do
really happen just once.

If I look hard enough
I can still see the scar

tracing its course across
me like a shooting star.

David Bart

Exit Now

An historic marker
and tombstones grow fluorescent
on the roadside, stern billboards
lit by the glaring video store.

The drive-thru girl flirts
with two weeks notice—a boy
who's never shaved wants
to save her from the Dairy Queen.

Pages from Bible coloring books
tint the windows of Sunday school,
thorns and scourging softened
with crayon and manila.

The Rock and Bowl marquee
says 9/11—we will never forget
Saturday is 2 for 1.

Most everyone is in before dark,
unaffected by this virulent Spring,
a muffled detonation of lust and pollen.

Others go into the night
elated or circumspect,
drawn by April's chilled nectar,
warm sidewalks, a nodding flagpole.

From the highway, sodium vapor glows.
Maybe this will be the night
things begin to change.
One car in three hours,
the exit ramp is a narrow hope.

Then a long, steel glimmer and exhausted roar.
A dual row of heads,
dwarfed and hazy
in the broad glass of a Greyhound.

REGRETS ONLY

Now that my mother's gone,
I wake from my silky sleep
regretting that old mattress she
spent so many years upon
how hard it must have felt
against her riddled mind
and withered body.

Why didn't I buy her
a feather bed
a goose down duvet
Egyptian cotton sheets
so cool and sleek
she might have slid into slumber
and a pillow so soft
she might have imagined
she was already in heaven?

Why didn't I pipe forties music—
the kind she jitter-bugged to
during the war—
into that south bedroom
where she lay day after day
while the people she once loved
gazed down on her from the west wall,
the faded yellow photos the one right note,
for which I can take no credit,

except for being among them.

GONE

Lately, I've been dreaming
of losing my purse.
The strap is snatched
from my shoulder
as I walk down the street,
or lifted from a chair
at a restaurant table.
Perhaps, I've been careless,
left it unwatched in a grocery cart
as I scanned the shelves or
abandoned in a corner
at a social gathering,
vulnerable to a swipe by
an unsavory sort.
I am seized with panic,
overwhelmed with helplessness
as my driver's license, checkbook,
credit cards, and family photos,
the data of my existence,
are stripped away.

I shudder into wakefulness
and sink with relief to find it
steadfast in its place
at my bedside on the floor.
And in morning light, I consider
as I edge closer to the horizon
if the notion of disappearing
has begun to weigh in.

Carolyn Praytor Boyd

NOT YOUR COMMON FOOT FETISH

Lady's got pretty feet
Long, lean, bony ends
Strapped in Manolo Blahniks

All day stilettos go
Rub skin to skin
Standing tippy-toe, tap, tap
Ankles roll little circles
Things not going her way

Now, Baby has pinky toes
Like little grubs, live
Each one sweet toys
Grow up someday
Grow up some way

Mama got broad feet
Spread out like a river
Overflow the sole
Tiny razor cross leather
Right over workaday callous
Lets it breathe

When these feet stamp
Sand sprays a hundred miles
Dance round a fire in Arabia
Dance to a radio in Selma
Dance right out of those glass slippers

GOD IS HONEY

I see my great-grandmother
in her village where

Winter
is a fang.

I see her turn to me on the November road.
At 19, she gives me a cold, wild grin.
She gives me a smile that is
not smoke. She clutches birds in
her fists. Black birds she
has killed in the desiccated
forest. They are hanging
upside down—blood
flowing to the skull
which she eats, alone
with her big mouth.

She nails the dark wings
over the door in a flying
pattern. She says God's Angels

Don't come here—you are
too high. I suck my
honey from a dry tree where it

Does me like an ocean.

LIKE FATHER

My father's embrace is tighter
Now that he knows
He is not the only man in my life.
He whispers, *Remember when,* and, *I love you,*
As he holds my hand hungry
For a discussion of Bible scriptures
Over breakfast. He pours cups of coffee
I can't stop
Spilling.

My father's embrace is firm and warm
Now that he knows. He begs forgiveness
For anything he may have done to make me
Turn to abomination
As he watches my eggs, scrambled
Soft. Yolk runs all over the plate.
A rubber band binds the morning paper.

My father's embrace tightens. Grits
Stiffen. I hug back
Like a little boy, gripping
To prove his handshake.
Daddy squeezes me close,
But I cannot feel his heartbeat
And he cannot hear mine—
There is too much flesh between us,
Two men in love.

PRAYER OF THE BACKHANDED

Not the palm, not the pear tree
Switch, not the broomstick,
Nor the closest extension
Cord, not his braided belt, but God,
Bless the back of my daddy's hand
Which, holding nothing tightly
Against me and not wrapped
In leather, eliminated the air
Between itself and my cheek.
Make full this dimpled cheek
Unworthy of its unfisted print
And forgive my forgetting
The love of a hand
Hungry for reflex, a hand that took
No thought of its target
Like hail from a blind sky,
Involuntary, fast, but brutal
In its bruising. Father, I bear the bridge
Of what might have been
A broken nose. I lift to you
What was a busted lip. Bless
The boy who believes
His best beatings lack
Intention, the mark of the beast.
Bring back to life the son
Who glories in the sin
Of immediacy, calling it love.
God, save the man whose arm
Like an angel's invisible wing
May fly backward in fury
Whether or not his son stands near.
Help me hold in place my blazing jaw
As I think to say excuse me.

Robert Burlingame

Los Chisos

(an event of 1856, Big Bend, Texas)

The stones cry out.
He smokes his last cigarette.
All the others wet.

And listens.
To the stones. While heat rips the river.
Water taken in sadness. Old men talk.

There were oaks at the river.
And rocks. Rocks of sixty million years.
Lichened.
                    They brought the girl here.
Made her ride a hard horse through miles of mesquite.
Made her get down. Let her bathe.

Dumb phallus over the slow stream.
Horses pissing in the dirt.
Girl's father at the ranch. His throat gashed.

Now. Only winds and old men.
The bandits long gone. Cheated of their girl.
One Maria. Afloat. Dead in the water. Her breasts flat.
And no sky watching.

CROWS

The boys are hungry
the boys are circling:

the boys are singing
their anthem in the dark

where there is no shame:

there is not enough
there's never enough.

The road shines tonight
to blind all the stars

and the floor lights up
a storm of painted eyes:

the boys watch closely
the boys will fluster.

It is the same furious
dance over and again.

The boys don't mind
the boys won't cry

and if they're crying
they're crying *more*

Joseph Campana

DAY LADY

for Nina Simone (1933-2003)

My rusted pipe can't hold her
tone, her gold: it's 3am, it's
already. Time comes. What ever
cannot cut is voice: the sheaf
that binds the scythe. I also hate
where I rise from, sometimes.
Come back. Every note blossoms:
amber: tears of waves of grain.
You have rooted my river. I
pass and under. I burn, I burn
to cool you to voice and cry
to sky Paris and the sky crying
song her: would that: I did.

WOLF

Little man, I said, keep the wolf
from my door: one more night,

one more wretched night and day.
The wolf said *wait* and the season

was packing its bags but it would
not leave and it would never leave.

Little man, I said, there's a tooth
at my throat, and the tooth said

time and it was really a wolf and it
was cloaked in a sheep's skin of

satisfaction, and there was a fury
raining down at night and it tapped

at the windows. Little man, I said,
close the door there's a wolf in

the air and there is a fury that even
fear can't touch and it is gnawing

me, I feel it gnawing at me and
the wolf said *shelter* and I knew it

was a lie, I felt it as a lie I could
already feel its teeth tearing my skin.

Mary Margaret Carlisle

DIPPING CRAWDADS

in the bottom of a pebbled creek
fat crawdads dart under leaves
behind water-smoothed stones
and dive into whirling eddies
but daddy, in long black waders
nets slow and quick alike
and drops each squirmy catch
into a heavy aluminum bucket
held out of reach
by her laughing brother
she wants to help hold or net
but is told she is too small
next year will come her turn
she cannot see that far ahead
only into the clear fast creek
but even then she is convinced
she will always be too small
too young or not quite ready
her brother—first loved
so much brighter than the rest—
he will always hold the bucket
as everything dips into his hands

Cyrus Cassells

THE CROSSED-OUT SWASTIKA

At the spring's onset, imagine, there were fists
instead of fragrance,

barbarous, kestrel-swift bulletins,
April upon April hope braided

with arrests, betrayals,
dark as the derided

spaces in our censored mail.
The borders became

too-tight belts.
Watchtowers, garrisons, checkpoints,

daunting as gorgons,
proliferated —

while in a covert,
a Mephisto fury,

the ravenous
zeros of the ovens glowed —

In that time of brutal roll calls,
when our brusque, marauded world became

a labyrinth,
an egregious snare,

a burning meadow,
we grew accustomed

to the brunt of the words:
blitzkrieg, quisling,

as our prescient souls,
unalloyed Virgils,

impasse after impasse,
whispered on oarless days:

Can't you see?
This is the crucible:

your shoes, your cherished rings—
these will be confiscated,

and you yourself
may be whisked away—

In war-bred dreams, we nestled
beside bomb-jostled

bodies of compatriots, confreres,
our cradling breath

a berceuse—
grief-cloaked,

avid to construct,
instead of unappeasable jackboots,

an impervious forest
peppered with shots,

a truce-clean music.
In vehement dreams,

we endeavored
to awaken the dead,

to confess, unabashed:
Lampshades of sullied flesh, linens

fashioned of human hair—
we were not prepared,

we were not prepared to stand
outside humanity—

Sixty years:
that world-pain, that harrowing,

is hushed now,
the unseeing insist,

—pallid, nearly imponderable beneath
a mantle of obscuring mist

and standstill cobwebs:
the spiders' meticulous legacy.

And we, the gagged, the herded,
the disavowed,

the wholly haunted
and the ever-haunting,

answer, strophe and antistrophe:
in clarifying sun,

come see, inheritor,
come celebrate

the un-bossed bloom
of a crossed-out swastika,

come walk with us
in confounding Birkenau,

near the tumbledown dragons
of the old crematoria,

knowing everywhere you walk,
you are walking on human ash.

Auschwitz-Birkenau, November 1, 2005

Cyrus Cassells

THE SINGING FOREST

A red and ocher forest near Zilina,
was my earliest classroom,

my first wondrous library
and lavish sanctuary:

on hillsides,
pregnant with autumn,

my just-widowed mother and I
would dally and cull

plump wood-berries and wild mushrooms
for our supper.

As a tow-headed, willing boy,
I was taught to venerate

each forest thing,
singing in Slovak,

in the treble clef,
dobre, dobre

("good, good"),
as my spellbound eyes passed

from leaf to russet leaf,
branch to glistening branch.

Don't stray too far, son;
don't step on the wand of the vila,

the sweet-souled forest witch,
my solicitous mother would tease me—

So when the rum-fueled German
gestured and said,

do you hear that music?
That's the singing forest,

I was whisked, rabbit-quick,
to my childhood copse,

Mother's robust rendition
of *How Does the Czar Take His Tea?*,

to the stone ribs
of the flying castle of Lietava—

Amid the crows' tattooing caws,
I detected

a terrible braying,
then I glimpsed them

above the Nazi's spittle-bright
jest and helmet:

a row of men hooked
to dispiriting poles.

And suddenly I grasped:
my cry,

my unchecked agony
would be subsumed

by theirs:
an abject chorus—

Dangling,
ebbing, I imagined

Mother's consoling alto:
Quick, Slavo, focus

on the streak of the deer,
like an August star—

Then, in a moment's match-burst,
someone cut me down,

convinced I was a corpse,
but I was stubbornly alive—

And the immense light, the prevailing
singing that supplants crucifixion,

parted the forest.

Zilina, The Slovak Republic, 2005

GARDEN PARK, MICHIGAN, 1897

Nonchalant in the day,
the boy in the pointillist suit
crosses the Mathematical Bridge.
He has a book open in one hand,
three letters and a diary to mail.
He fails to notice the sun-shocked face of a soldier,
the mercenaries lunching by the hill.
Strolling a lane, Duchamp and Rothko argue
over the compromise of incantation.
It is, they say, derivative of necromancy, of alchemy.
If Seurat disagrees, he isn't saying.
His mistress is demanding more Bearnaise sauce, more song.
Barnett Newman details a piece for them:
melded to a Calvary stone
I see a clown and a waterfall, a cliff diver off his line.
The demands of nakedness and divinity
define us today, if not tomorrow.
Death finds a little corner in every work of art.
The boy's book is open and fluttering in the mineral winds.
One page is a kingfisher, another is a pear.

D. B. Cherry

DIPTYCH

*And Desire Shall Fail: Because Man Goeth to his Long Home and
Mourners Go About the Streets.*

Passports will lapse in the safety deposit box
and ignorance will become our strategy
though there can be no un-knowing
because heat transforms a thing;
our molecules quicken, we grow expansive.
When the heat has gone
we will wear our skin more loosely.
Desire will not cease as a heart ceases.
Its dying will not manifest as the cold
leeching upward through the veins
from genitals to heart to brain
Desire will die with hands sweeping the face
of a clock, or the earth.
A house or an omelet will burn.

Desirous of Communion with One of the Inscrutable Gods of the Orient

The India of the photograph is made of lead
and the sadhu is a weightless kind,
his skin seeming newly minted. He squats
before his beggar's bowl, his penis and scrotum
encased in a plaster gourd, his withered right arm
hanging over his head like a winter branch.
He had reached into the sky for God,
the knife in the cloudy dishwater.
Blood, lymph and eventually the scant moisture of bone
worked downward, the intermittent heart being
no match for an earth that bends even the sky toward itself.
The arm died cell by cell, each one singing its dying
until each was a raisin. Its sweetness condensed to lure God,
watching from the trees a leaden bird.

Mary Cimarolli

On the Road from Trujillo to Variadero

More coyotes than cars,
a windmill, deserted barn, stone house fallen to ruin,
distant ranch house, Longhorn skull,
Our Lady of the Rosary wayside shrine:
this endless ribbon of asphalt unfurls before me.

In a vast and barren world,
brown vistas narrow
as I focus on a simple white cross
draped with plastic roses
marking the spot where life ended hard by the pavement.

Passing a diminutive white church,
I see a small herd of ranchers
led by two weathered men in Sunday clothes
bearing a baby's white coffin into the chapel
topped with stark wooden cross.

Long ago, in another state,
the life of my teenage brother
ended just so,
and the sister who died before I was born
was so escorted into a small church.

Now, part of me remains on the road
from Trujillo to Variadero,
beside the plain white cross draped with plastic roses,
beside the weathered men in Sunday clothes
bearing a baby's white coffin into the chapel.

Sandra Cisneros

LOVE POEM #1

a red flag
woman I am
all copper
chemical
and you an ax
and a bruised
thumb

unlikely
pas de deux
but just let
us wax
it's nitro
egypt
snake
museum
zoo

we are
connoisseurs
and commandos
we are rowdy
as a drum
not shy like Narcissus
nor pale as plum

then it is I want to hymn
and hallelujah
sing sweet sweet jubilee
you my religion
and I a wicked nun

Sandra Cisneros

THE SO-AND-SO'S

Your other women are well-behaved.
Your magnolias and Simones.
Those with the fine brave skin like moon
and limbs of violin and bones like roses.
They bloom nocturnal and are done
with nary a clue behind them.
Nary a clue. Save one or two.

Here is the evidence of them.
Occasionally the plum print
of a mouth on porcelain.
And here the strands of mermaids
discovered on the bathtub shores.
And now and again, tangled in
the linen—love's smell—
musky, unmistakable,
terrible as tin.

But love is nouveau.
Love is liberal as a general
and allows. Love with no say so
in these matters, no X nor claim nor title,
shuts one wicked eye and courteously
abides.

I cannot out
with such civility.
I don't know how to
go—not mute as snow—
without my dust and clatter.
I am no so-and-so.
I who arrived deliberate as Tuesday
without my hat and shoes

with one rude black tattoo
and purpose thick as pumpkin.

One day I'll dangle
from your neck, public as a jewel.
One day I'll write my name on everything

as certain as a trail of bread.
I'll leave my scent of smoke.
I'll paint my wrists.
You'll see. You'll see.
I will not out so easily.

I was here. As loud as trumpet.
As real as pebble in the shoe.
A tiger tooth. A definite voodoo.

Let me bequeath
a single pomegranate seed,
a telltale clue.
I want to be like you. A who.

And let them bleed.

Kathleen Cook

THE SHUFFLE

I fell this morning
a shuffled foot over brick
raised by inconstant earth
that will not stay in

one place—like neighbor's cat
I was slowly evicting, the
one that wanted to eat
my cat's food put

on my decaying wooden
porch—wood rotting
from the rain of this
tropical clime, where

water has to keep
shuffling from earth to
sky; nothing staying
in place.

I fell flat over uneven
bricks; my knees breaking
the plane, my breath
adding to the water soaked

air and stars beyond skidding
clouds above me, which I,
carefully rolling over,
studied, contemplating my

possible brokenness or wholeness,
under a Buddha's Hand, when
a cat came and meowed
questioningly, as I resolved

to lie again in
that beautiful place
on cold bricks
under the stars.

SEGUIN

What did she
do in long summer
afternoons standing
inside the small,
square window

three houses over
from our house? Her
son faint
and washed out
in my memory

except for stiff,
blonde crew cut, a
small boy's
thin shoulders,
tanned elbows and knees.

Their house a white
wood shingle with no
front sidewalk.   No
husband we knew of
in our church or

at the nearby grocery.
Somehow I heard
she was from Seguin.
A place I didn't
know, a place I

forever linked
with a thin woman's
tall shadow in a house
I never entered.   The flat
plane of empty, the troubled

call for home.   A
starched white blouse
behind a high screened window
over an empty kitchen sink.

Sarah Cortez

SERIAL KILLER

Sometimes I remember how
he carted the bodies frozen
across interstate cement
in his truck's refrigerated maw.

Other times I see girls
like the ones he selected—
runaways already married
to danger, a past that bore

no repeating. Slender girls
with large dark eyes,
winsome above a boyish
flatness barely hinting

at a womanhood still
distant. What I pray
is that the first blow
was an outright kill.

That he wasn't too excited
to aim well and execute
swiftly before laying
each one out

inside his stainless tundra.
Rock-hard flesh and
frozen hair later
jettisoned into scrub

besides stagnant ditches
next to a highway's
curling cement ribbon
leading to the next

tender girl.

Maryke Cramerus

ETRUSCAN TOMBS

Rough steps slope down, ash gray, to the unlit tomb.
Heavy metal doors are bolted shut. Black glass
shows nothing, does not reflect. Push the button:
a stone room flares: maroon, turquoise, edged in black.
Lions, spotted leopards crouch, blue deer leap up
over acrobats, shoving wrestlers, dancers
who sway, hands dangling above their heads—the starved
dog, hooded pershu and his executioner.

The dead, man and wife, recline, torsos upright,
not yet led from their last banquet. They still lift
flat wine cups—smiling at guests who drink amid
garlanded trees, hunt duck, wild boar. Behind them
the she-demon Vanth waits, black-winged, with her key
at the painted door. Her bronze torch will light them down.

Stan Crawford

AFTER READING ABOUT THE DEATH OF KEN LAY AND CONSULTING ORWELL AND BALZAC

I scrutinize my morning face,
all folds and puffs.
Hair slack, gray-streaked,
random as straw.
A balcony of skin beneath each eye.

At fifty we have the face we deserve.
I too must be guilty of something.

Near Embarcadero a homeless man
with dreadlocks tangled as CIA plots
defies the signs that forbid feeding pigeons
and scatters his scraps of illicit bread.

Disheveled panhandlers and skateboard punks
hang on Haight Street and litter the park
with detritus of undertow
drenched in gold light.

Behind every great fortune, a crime.
A prison placed near the golden gate.
Sour inextricable from sweet
inside the chambers of our grapefruit hearts.

Carolyn Dahl

THE WOMAN CAME OUT

The woman came out of her house
hands filled with butterflies.
He meant to look away.
She was still in her night gown.
He was a migrant worker
fixing the roof across the street,
dressed in stained clothes, a towel
under his cap to protect his neck
from the morning's burning sun.

But how could he not stare
when she raised her arms
and from her fingertips
butterflies flew like orange
castanets of light?

It was as if he had never
seen anything fly. As if a butterfly
could be God or his pre-born self.
He would have kneeled in her fluttering
rooms had she called, but the door closed.

Standing against the sky,
balancing on bare house beams,
a plywood sheet raised above his
head and tilted into the wind,
he never felt so light. Knowing
what he knew of faith, he had
only to step off the edge to
glide on heavy wings, turn to the sun
and follow the butterflies home.

DEPRESSION

Hunger moved in
with its truck loads of sleepless hours.
It went to bed with many children.
They said economy was real depressed.
Bureaucrats blamed telephone poles
for staring at the moon,
blamed the moon
for being tardy,
blamed the wind
for being stubborn.
From tall buildings you could see people
lying prone in parking lots
and you imagined their deaths as
pale stars falling on the black
asphalt of poor neighborhoods
and you saw their bodies as
footnotes, as asterisk markers shining
at the bottom of a story
no one wanted to read.

André de Korvin

THE PASSPORT

When my father spoke French with his heavy Russian accent,
syllables rolled off his tongue
like explosions rocking the outskirts of Kiev
in the winter of '17
when at the beginning of each day
the sun slowly rose
in the sky, a clenched fist.
I remember his smile stretching across the passport's faded pages,
the top part of his head
buried by official stamps that said
no entry, no future, no exit, no past.

ON A BALCONY IN CENTRAL SPAIN

Searing sun
Coming storm
A bird on a line
and me,
eyes on the mountains
hands on the rail

Bird flies
Lightning strikes
first far
then close,
and I watch,
taking comfort in the thought
that I can see, can hear
a storm greater than
the one I carry inside,
standing quietly on the
balcony of a home
in a land that is not yet
and may never be
just that,
just this,
my home

Bird flies
I stand
the storm
inside

Carol Denson

ALL TIME IS PRESENT

All time is present. The past thumps in the heart,
floats through the veins. You can step into the same river twice
when you are the river, when one gray sky becomes another
and though your body is enclosed in a red truck at a stoplight
you are really walking down a Chicago sidewalk in winter,
it's always winter and your heart can break over and over and
        over
until you come to love the breaking, the glimmer of sunlight
        on icy water.

When the river is you, you're nine riding a bike no hands
        singing hallelujah,
seventeen meeting the boy with muscles under the gray shirt
you're unbuttoning before he's completely shut the front door,
        twenty-three wondering
and amazed that life is like *this*, and suddenly you awake on a
        porch in Houston
seeing the trees stretch their bare limbs against the sky
while your boyfriend approaches, walking that way he walked
that meant he loved you and you loved him
and there that fact was and what did one do with it. It is always
that moment too.

In winter, it is always winter and all winters, these limbs
will always spread motionless against the sky
and you will always be approaching down the sidewalk
where my life lives, and I will always be alone in Chicago
walking and walking, my heart breaking, my soul alive
because it hurt so much I could finally feel something.
It is not always until it is gone, when the images roar
and emblazon themselves until I cannot see
and so turn to them blindly, embracing their shadows.
"Don't wait for me," I tell them, "I'm not coming back.
I love you. I'm sorry."

Marco A. Domínguez

THE BLUE JAY

My hand isn't small enough
to fit inside its ribcage,
so Erika reminds me
she is the girl, the one
that found it huddled
by a strand of fence.

So I hand it back, open
and red. She whispers
how warm and little
the lungs feel. The heart
is an almond and her hand
is gone, up to the knuckles.

I want to feel what's inside,
but Erika won't let go
and it starts to rain.
She tells me how its bones
scratch her skin.
And she wants me
to take the bird and pull it

off her hand. I grasp
the feathers it has left
on its drenched wings,
but the rain is too much.
We need to dry. To cross
the fence and hide under trees
until the rain passes.

At the base of a pine,
the blue jay on her lap stains
her sundress. She tells
how its insides cool like night air.

She wants to go home
and I want to dislodge
those lungs from her fingers,
break the ribs around her hand,
and bury the bird,
but these pines do little
and the rain sticks her hair
to her face.

Erika says she hates the blue jay
first, and me second.
That we're the reason
her hand will scar.
I tell her something between
sorry and it's my fault,
and she ignores it, staring
at these pines, at these scattered
blue feathers.

THE GREEN GOOSE

When the goose
grew
green,
I knew
it wasn't a dream.
I observed
the emerald
bird.

The peculiar goose
hopped,
like a barefoot boy
on a hot sidewalk,
out of the pond

              bellowing

                    running so fast

                         he looked like a cyclist

pedaling toward a little
girl's dangling hand
holding tooth-marked
bread.

The terrified child

              ran

                  for shelter

                    behind a lattice fence.

The girl didn't
understand
the green goose's
plan.

For weeks and weeks
the green goose
                    chased
                            crackers and bread
wanting
to be
fed.

Returning to the
lettuce-laden lake,
the green goose
ate
lettuce-leaf
greens.

(It seems teens
plucked
Romaine
from their ham and cheese
tossing green kites
to the water.)

So you see,
the green goose
wasn't mean.
He knew
geese
weren't meant
to grow
green.

B. H. Fairchild

A PHOTOGRAPH OF THE *TITANIC*

When Travis came home from the monastery,
the ground had vanished beneath him,
and he went everywhere in bare feet

as if he were walking on a plane of light,
and he spoke of his sleepless nights
and of a picture in *National Geographic:*

a pair of shoes from the *Titanic* resting
on the ocean floor.   They were blue
against a blue ground and a black garden

of iron and brass.   The toes pointed outward,
toward two continents, and what had been
inside them had vanished so completely

that he imagined it still there, with the sea's
undersway bellying down each night
as each day after compline he fell into

his bed, the dark invisible bulk of tons
pushing down on the shoes, nudging them
across the blue floor, tossing them aside

like a child's hands in feverish sleep
until the shoe strings scattered and dissolved.
Sometimes he would dream of the shoes

coming to rest where it is darkest,
after the long fall before we are born,
when we gather our bodies around us,

when we curl into ourselves and drift
toward the little sleep we have rehearsed
again and again as if falling we might drown.

Mrs. Hill

I am so young that I am still in love
with Battlecreek, Michigan: decoder rings,
submarines powered by baking soda,
whistles that only dogs can hear. Actually,
not even them. Nobody can hear them.

Mrs. Hill from next door is hammering
on our front door shouting, and my father
in his black and gold gangster robe lets her in
trembling and bunched up like a rabbit in snow
pleading, *oh I'm so sorry, so sorry,*
so sorry, and clutching the neck of her gown
as if she wants to choke herself. *He said*
he was going to shoot me. He has a shotgun
and he said he was going to shoot me.

I have never heard of such a thing. A man
wanting to shoot his wife. His wife.
I am standing in the center of a room
barefoot on the cold linoleum, and a woman
is crying and being held and soothed
by my mother. Outside, through the open door
my father is holding a shotgun,
and his shadow envelops Mr. Hill,
who bows his head and sobs into his hands.

A line of shadows seems to be moving
across our white fence: hunched-over soldiers
on a death march, or kindly old ladies
in flower hats lugging grocery bags.

At Roman's Salvage tire tubes
are hanging from trees, where we threw them.
In the corner window of Beacon Hardware there's a sign:
WHO HAS 3 OR 4 ROOMS FOR ME. SPEAK NOW.
For some reason Mrs. Hill is wearing mittens.
Closed in a fist, they look like giant raisins.
In the *Encyclopaedia Britannica Junior*
the great Pharoahs are lying in their tombs,
the library of Alexandria is burning.
Somewhere in Cleveland or Kansas City
the purple heart my father refused in WWII
is sitting in a Muriel cigar box
and every V-Day someone named Schwartz
or Jackson gets drunk and takes it out.

In the kitchen now Mrs. Hill is playing
gin rummy with my mother and laughing
in those long shrieks that women have
that make you think they are dying.

I walk into the front yard where moonlight
drips from the fenders of our Buick Dynaflow.
I take out my dog whistle. Nothing moves.
No one can hear it. Dogs are asleep all over town.

Carolyn Tourney Florek

THE PARACHUTE OF INSIGHT

Is it a mere coincidence that insight follows insidious—
seemingly benign neighbors in the Webster's New College
dictionary—or is this serendipity just the way it is,
the fates in the minds of Noah and his successors meeting
and making this decision based on the logical
determining order of the alphabet?

And is it "an elucidating glimpse" to see one neighbor,
the one named Insidious, through the eyes of the other
named Insight? To see this ubiquitous dorm-mate popping
up all over campus, at every party, in every class, like spam
or Viagra on the Internet, or viral like smallpox, invisible
in the soft, comfortable blankets white-man gave red-man?

At first glance Insidious looks attractive, exciting, dynamic;
wears the latest fashions, knows all the best jokes, is the hot "it"
party guest. Later in Twelve Step 101 he/she is there, of course,
the most interesting person in the group, with incredible true
stories—practically epic—at once hilarious and heart
    wrenching.

Some mornings, when the sky is that perfect blue, after a
thunderstorm's blown away all the petrochemical grunge, I
release the parachute of insight, catching myself midair over
a beautiful earth, where even urban sprawl is tamed into
a quiet impressionistic order, peaceful from high up, with
glistening buildings, and neat patterns of homes, the cars and
trucks like purposeful ants moving on the reasonable grids of
streets and highways. And no visible sign of trash, no
messy details from up here, or indications of
things gone wrong in insidious-land. I see only
the backyard pools flashing like turquoise, the retinas of
my eyes sending this pleasurable color to my brain, as

I drift down like a dandelion seed, feeling my first impressions whisk by in the wind pressing against my whole being as I hope for a good and safe place to plant myself.

LACASSINE, PERHAPS

It's a simple question.
Simple as writing the last line of a poem,
or entering the date of a friend's death
in a book you borrowed but never returned.
One night my wife asks,
"Have you thought about
where you would like to be buried?"
And I say, "Yes." And she stays
silent for a long time.
I imagine she is waiting.
So am I.

I think about trees twisted ugly,
lean dogs dead in the empty streets,
orphaned by Hurricane Rita.
I think of earth turned over by grinding waves,
marble statues rubbed clean by wind,
then scoured by rags of dirt.
I wonder if the houses I once occupied survived,
and if they did not, was the rubble carted away
and laid to rest in unfamiliar earth.
Houses love their lots, I'm almost sure,
and regret the removal of their boards or bricks.

If there is a clean cemetery left
anywhere in Southwest Louisiana,
find it for me, buy a berth
for my body's final future.
Store me near magnolia trees
undaunted by rumors of foul weather.
Let me go, let me go
under, where no turning will touch me,
and no moon will wake me
in the middle of my dream.

Larry L. Fontenot

MOWING DECONSTRUCTED

The woman across the street ties back her hair,
puts on an old gray shirt when she mows.
As she circles her lot, crescents of sweat
grow huge under her arms and a dark patch
slowly spreads between her breasts
like a shadow drawn out after midday.

This shape reveals more than separation.
It conjures the lure of heat, suggests
a stance against grass and marriage.
I watch as her duel with nature becomes
a feud broken off only when the sun
begins to thin in the air of dusk.

Some nights when her man comes to visit,
I cross the street and stand outside her house.
I listen to her soft moan, the sound of sheets
stripped from the bed, the creak of bodies falling in.
She knows this about me, and teases
with an open window even when it's cold.

She has carefully constructed a boundary
that says this is me and this is you and we
will never share desire across this dark patch,
never speak in anxious tones, never meet
in the crux of a major crisis, have first names
or pretend to teach when we are really learning.

So I watch while she mows, step outside to retrieve
the paper, wave back when she raises one hand
to greet me, that splendid loop of moisture widening
like a mouth, a wound, an orb of love I will never know,
just fantasy held close, like the notion of climbing
through her window one night when she's alone.

Priscilla Frake

QUARTER MOON

The moon keeps losing pieces of itself.
Now it's down to its final quarter,
curved along the thinning inner edge
that is ridding itself to the dark.

> There was a battered Smith Corona
> in the room where my mother lay dying.
> We talked to fill the silence
> while Melissa played in the corner,
>
> and Amy typed.
> As my children left with my husband,
> Amy put these words in her grandmother's hands:
> "Don't think I'll remember nothing but this."

Four am. Driving to the airport.
Tracks and alleys, narrow streets,
not many street lamps.
Surely lost—

But we went on
following the detour,
the way behind in darkness.
Ahead—at last—thank God—the road.

> My mother's eyes were exact and fierce
> as I gave her my promise
> to do for them what she would do:
> to buy them dresses soon, for Easter.

Now it's time for them to board
and leave me to the moon's waning.
They get up, gripping each other's hands,
and go on.

She closed her eyes, then opened them
to say, "And shoes."

TODAY

I stared into my refrigerator
Like I was looking for the Second Coming.
All I saw were bits and pieces
Of previous meals.
The leftover shrimp from Pappa's,
Half a jar of niçoise olives,
Couple glasses of wine left in the bottle,
A little cheese, some seedless black grapes.
Bottled water seemed to be the only
Item in abundance. Clear, cool,
Bottled in sanitary conditions,
Totally tasteless.

Edwin Gallaher

ON THE WAY TO WORK

The chalk drawings on the sidewalk are gone.
They weren't worried away by rain either.
The concrete still keens to be marked on,
but like all youth the young man is gone.

Scribbles once revealed great self-expression:
clown masks, graffiti, a gun ship, a pawn.
Not disciplined by whims of weather,
the chalk drawings on the sidewalk are gone.

Deduct me from the scene. For years I've known
identities flit like moths in a sweater.
Wind can't whisk away knees pinning a lawn.
And young men aren't boys. Ever.

Jeannie Gambill

DIRECTIVE

TO A GROWN DAUGHTER

When you ride your motorcycle
wear your helmet.
Not the half helmet.
Wear your full helmet
always.
When you go out on your motorcycle
take only streets
where
there are no cars
no trucks
no buses
no other moving vehicles.
Do not go out in the rain.
Never on the freeways.
When you decide instead
to go on your bicycle
be faithful to all of these
instructions. The routes
you've shown us you take to work
through neighborhoods
on your bicycle, there are
cars parked on these narrow
streets. Be careful. It's hard
to see you.
Your motorcycle surely lost
from view when you are in traffic.
Do not go into the traffic.
Do not go anyplace where
there is danger. Stay
blocks away from any vehicle
in which the driver

is un-focused. Please say
you will do these things.
When you train on the highways
in the hills   when you want
the challenge   need the long
stretch   the cumulative miles
when you bike into the hills
when you take your bicycle
round the curve   slow
on the upward incline
and   down   down   gaining speed
the curve   go round the curve
go round and down the hill's
curve   not too fast.
When you line it out
the song of you
adhere please
to this
entreaty.

Lewis Garvin

CURATORIAL MANNERS

Two freezes only nights apart, not the usual
Houston winter, and plants can sit a week

or two, removed from light in hibernation,
around the Chinese rug. The larger ones

extend above the gardens of worn yarn,
geometric flowers filled with dirt (and dust

mites) down through knots once tied by knowing hands.
This season's leaves enrich the ancient petals,

plump and orange and open on their stems
as long as wool endures. A mountain looms

in brown above a thirsty tiger at
a stream that moves as quickly as his life.

The ficus droops and falls into his world,
particles of dust and leaf by shriveled

letting go to join the Ideal always
there. In a valley grove where leaves stay fleshed,

if not this Tiger, then Another, pauses,
bends, and drinks again from constant water.

Wayne Lee Gay

CONCORD DISCORD

Blinded by his own morning star,
Yearning for gods disguised as farm boys
        Henry David writes of Amos, Abner, Elnathan
And thirsts for a smile, a greeting, a touch.
Hairy-necked, wide-eyed, word-worn Henry David
Hides his hunger
        with praise of trees and fungus.

The good folk of Concord forgive him his rambling in the wood
And the musical scratching of his pen.
He's ugly but pure, and reads so many books,
          he must be good,
            the townsfolk say.

Then the handyman arrives.

Handsome Alek, swaggering house to house, fixing doors,
    chopping wood,
        igniting desires.
A prince with a hammer,
The townsfolk say.
        He lingers
          a little longer,
            a little more often

At Henry David's house.

How brief, how deep, how long we drown in a pond of words.

Till, torn by years, and the shame of love, and Alek's drunken
     pranks and wanderings,
Henry David turns on the prince.

Go home and cut your throat, he says.

Emerson, intrigued, bemused, scribbles in his journal.
Blind for once, he doesn't see Henry David, wordless
(   ) alone, silent, sobbing.

Wayne Lee Gay

TO A DRAG QUEEN

> *Our life is and will remain essentially mysterious...*
> —*Flannery O'Connor*

I.

The silk dress, the spike heels, the black lashes,
The savage-red lips,
The hint of cleavage,
        the carefully tucked
                cock,
Smooth and flat under the pink silk.

Everything's perfect. Everything's a lie.

Looking at the mirror, before you go on,
You smile, and dabble
        one wet drop of perfume
                on your shoulder.

You can change a flat tire in two minutes,
      fix anything that's broke.
You've got jeans, workboots, running shorts at home in the
    closet,
You laughed when you got chosen last in eighth-grade p.e.
    class,
      then cried, just a little, when you got home.
But when you look in the mirror, sometimes Careesa the
    Queen of the Night smiles back,
And says
    Everything's all right now.

Even the song, lipsyncing love and longing,
Even the ladylike blush when the man at the mike makes dirty
    jokes,
Even the perfume
        no one but you can smell.

II.

I'm just standing at the bar, see, cruising, looking for a little
fun for the night, just checking out the boys. This cute little
guy strolls by. Jeans, boots. Smiles, says *Hello.* I say *Hello* back.
He stops, comes right over to me, starts talking. Practically
tells me his life story. We start making out. He starts talking
about me and him going over to his place. Right then. Then he
mentions that he does shows. By which he means drag shows.
I'm Careesa the Queen of the Night, he says. He sees me back off.
Shows are shows, he says. *I'm all boy when I go home. Come home
with me and let me show you.* Flashes white teeth, so pretty.
Bright brown eyes, so fine. *I shave this off when I do shows,* he
says, stroking his sweet little goatee.

III.

Two cats roll across my naked body
                while I watch you undress.
You're all boy, no lie.
Flat, smooth, hard man-chest.
And just a tiny taste of perfume
             when you stretch out next to me.

John Gorman

SOUTHWEST FL 439: HOUSTON/HOBBY-EL PASO

When we sink, at last,
from El Nino-driven clouds,
one look at the rolling, arroyo-eaten
yellow-tan pelt of the land
and my eyes go slitty.
My skin, which, in its real life Irish stubbornness
never tans, turns to a whisky-and-water
topographic duplicate of what I'm seeing again
now, first time in twelve years.
Muscle sliding lethally on bone,
I shift in my seat, belt loosely fastened,
and wonder will I be able to pick up a pump-action
at the airport souvenir shop. Riding
(I'll need a horse, too, of course) into that barrenness
with a bedroll, canteen, shells strapped
crisscross—it's ammo, after all,
that makes the difference—*bandolero*
or patrol boy—seems the only thing to do.
        A conclusion
which dissipates, a little, in the hotel van
among expensively irrigated landscaping,
shoppers' traffic getting the jump on the weekend,
the Peter Piper Pizzeria. Once in my plastic
nametag, I settle for the Cormac McCarthy sessions.
The people there are intense.
They wear darker colors than the other
academics. Their cheekbones are more pronounced.
They laugh, a little uneasily, at their
obsession with slow fuses, sudden murder. They update
each other's URL's. This is the sort
of compromise that makes the middle class
so unkillable. Yet the brutality
of West Texas, Las Cruchean New Mexico, riverine

Chihuahua is real enough—the sunbitten context
of everything—hard and powdery,
mined, teeming with weaponed life forms.
The McCarthy scholars, of course, are also
theologians, as the desert, of course, also
casts up these ampitheatrical mountains
on both sides of what,
for a while, will be the border
to gleam like visible seraphim in the lifegiving
killer sun.
        Nothing,
I notice, has sorted itself out for me here
any more than it does in Galveston.
Ambiguity, the Conference Chair might say,
In the Emerging Literatures of the Southwest.

Jennifer Grotz

ALCHEMY

All day the city went on being a city
we traversed as if it could be conquered by touch,

leaning against stone walls and wrapping our fingers
around rails overlooking the river.

And all through the city, the day went on being a day
blazing ruthlessly, even when it started to rain,

and the devil beat his daughter all afternoon
until sparrows stirred the cauldron of sky

and dusk doused the flames in greenish smoke.
That was more or less the recipe to make night,

when the city writes its unspendable wealth inside us.
When a pebble becomes a bright coin on the sidewalk,

where a black ermine scurries under a car
to replace motor oil rushing into the gutter.

And I become a bird squeezed in a boy's dirty palms
while you digest an iron egg of dread,

the empirical result whenever moonlight
takes shadow to be her lawfully wedded husband.

One's fate in this city is to come and become and be overcome.
In each of us a mad rabbit thrashes and a wolf pack howls.

THE WOODSTOVE

The woodstove is banked to last the night,
its slim legs, like an elegant dog's, stand obediently
on the tile floor while in its belly a muffled tumult
cries like wind keening through the hemlocks.

Human nature to sleep by fire, and human nature
to be sleepless by it, too. I get up to watch
the blue flames finger soft chambers in the wood
while the coals swell with scintillating breaths.

What made Rousseau once observe that dogs will not
build fires? (And further, that in the pleasing warmth
of a fire already started, they will not add wood?)
What is it to be human? to forge connection,

to make interpretations of fire and contain them
in a little iron stove? And what is it to be fire?
To burn with indifference, to consume
the skin of the arm as easily as the bark of a log.

Sleepy warmth begins to fill the room in which
life wants to live and fire wants to burn,
the room which in the morning
will hold a fire changed to cooling ash.

Outside, smoke escapes and for an instant
mirrors nature, too, the way falling snow
reveals the wind's mind, and change of mind,
before world and mind grow inscrutable again.

Laurie A. Guerrero

LAS LENGUAS

Once, a man told me
to hear the voice of God
one must first be able to speak
in tongues.

Years later, another man
told me speaking in tongues
was the kind of sin
you couldn't hide.

Who knows what the priests
told my mother when, with a quivering
chin, she pleaded *Por favor, padre,*
necesito it al baño, squeezing
her tiny thighs together
in the best English
she could muster.

William F. Guest

WHY GO?

O minney moe miney
Might flu the ruke—
Not terra not luna but una:
O round such time as ends and overs,
O cross the null aleaping,
O thru the zoom aflum from ever
Where end and 'gin twincircle so sadly.

Why go moe so miney to any?
Lux and larn oercome the stickers;
And vision as misty as monsoons weeping
Soon creeping to coffin is kinder.
All morn's asun and dark's atwinkle
And green's so furious it dies abeing . . .
Why go moe when staying's so sticking?

Never have you seen such always nothing . . .
Great suns are quenched by simply not being.
Go on around where Lucifer faltered,
Breeze past God's old nursery nook:
End is so lost and time's no longer . . .
Go on moe and miney be with you.

RUSH

It sprang forth at sundown and was gone—
flash of dark motion, leggy,
black winding stripe of a tail—
so fast I couldn't see its face
only the red-brown blur of its body.

Now, at the place on the road
where the bobcat leapt
I slow down and look
each time I pass
hoping to see it again or another.

I come to the country, I say,
for the unhurried pace and solitude.
But, sometimes,
there is a bolt of life so unexpected,
so intoxicating

that I think
This is what propels me.
This and, then, desire for a better look.

Michelle Hartman

SHALLOW OBSERVATIONS

there's a woman in a nursing home, on the outskirts of town
believes when she dies Ernest Tubb is gonna come and Waltz
    her across Texas
'cept Ernest ain't coming, 'cause he bought into the whole
    Heaven fantasy package
so death is to be survived
and survivors are not attractive
rarely possessed with pert butts or high saucy breasts
thus tight little women standing next to me in the grocery
    store
don't bother when the big one comes they'll be raped
    repeatedly
by marauding hordes
while the ugly will handle serviceable tasks
in a world where souls pay forty dollars
to stand in hundred degree heat at Six Flags, three screaming
    children
but resent standing in line at the DMV
sixteen dollars gets you a license to drive on Dallas freeways
where you'll promptly be killed
'cause Johnny can't speed
and the last sign you saw was clean dirt wanted
Zen'll get you through the heat, this too shall pass
but brother, it'll pass faster with a work boot up it's ass
providing said hole comes with more teeth than tattoos
unless you're in parts of this great land
where a man with all his teeth is the equivalent of a
    leprechaun
so if you find one buy a lottery ticket it's your lucky day
but if all else fails play dead, it's working for the Indians
while the black man demands reparations and the old woman
    just smiles
asks him if whitey pays what he owes then what'll he give the
    Indians in back rent

that is if he takes time from celebrating a Christmas no one
    enjoys
and it's time to announce the holiday emperors naked
so you kill his money dreams
discover the difference between a serial killer and an
    executioner is a benefits package
'cept stealing if you don't already have money is a perilous
    thing,
means you're a democrat and if you're not my religion you're
    going to hell
course my address is already 4401 handbasket
and I'm just a crazy woman in a big gold dress but when I die
      when I die . . .
Willie Nelson is gonna pick me up in Honeysuckle Rose
we'll smoke doobies the size of summer sausages
heading into the sunset
      we're gonna . . . ride . . . ride . . . ride.

Kurt Heinzelman

JACOBUS VREL

In the room a woman sits, in profile,
looking through a door, a thing that one
can do, in Holland, for the top half's open.
Another woman, mostly arm, is framed
by shadow, *die frau ohne schatten.*
But, no. It's not Bayreuth. We want to
keep this scene Dutch, and not alone
because of those stiff ear-flapped bonnets —
it's also the dipthongs, the fruity labials,
impastoed here like strokes of light.
Dividing the room is a wooden screen
that leaves another room inside,
the curtain across it pulled back. A fire
in the hearth to the lower right seems
scarcely more than a paint scratch.
By contrast, the fire tongs beside it
are Dürer-correct, the sunspot
on the bell jar intense as the lilies
at Giverny. An ellipsis of plates
orbits the room, each the color of
full moons at dawn. The woman's chair
has sloping arms and shortened legs —
a nursing chair, it's called — and she
has fabric spread across her lap,
which at first it seems she's mending,
but no, her chin's in one hand, the other's
underneath the . . . whatever it is.
A quilt? Because she's chilled? Because
the door is open wide (on top)
and a fire like that can't warm a room
like this? Because in Holland sunshine's
fool's gold? Because there is so much
we can't take in — the leaf-mold smell

105

of nursing, say, and folded linen, light
that is everywhere and nowhere,
invisible as drapery, filling up
a room that, really, probably is being
aired out, perhaps for the first time
all winter, a room that has been signed

Jacobus Vrel

a man known to us now only
because, in an epoch we have named
Vermeer's, he signed his own small
patchwork quilt of oils like these—
a man whose story lives, as stories do,
if they do, by reaching one good
arm out, the other wrapped tightly
about its own chiaroscura.

> *After the painting usually called*
> *"The Little Nurse." Nothing is known*
> *of the artist besides his signature*
> *on some 30 paintings.*

Jesse G. Herrera

MI QUERIDA PASTEL,

How delicious a morsel
Of any of my recollections
Of you wrapped in your
Perfume and nothing more,
Con su piel, your touch, tu pelo,
Your breathe, right down to your
Little toe, the delectable taste of you
on the tongue of my thoughts of you,
Con todo mi cariño—mi amore

For Trish

RAPTORS

They hover over their beers
with eyes like feathered talons
poised to stroke or tear
ready to defer or grasp
knowing you are gringo
knowing this is Cuzco
knowing you are alone and very alive
that you are a cuy braving the sun
in a valley between brown peaks
You are rich
You are ripe
You are free
and they have seen you many times before
tasted your strange ways
tested your transient strength
Their hunger created Tahuantinsuyo
the four corners of the world
They ate valley after valley
absorbing culture after culture
building one empire
now resisting another
They have not eaten in four hundred years
They know they will be here forever
They are two slender dark-haired women
very pretty
sitting in a bar
watching music videos
and watching
your eyes
move

Edward Hirsch

BRANCH LIBRARY

I wish I could find that skinny, long-beaked boy
who perched in the branches of the old branch library.

He spent the Sabbath flying between the wobbly stacks
and the flimsy wooden tables on the second floor,

pecking at nuts, nesting in broken spines, scratching
notes under his own corner patch of sky.

I'd give anything to find that birdy boy again
bursting out into the dusky blue afternoon

with his satchel of scrawls and scribbles,
radiating heat, singing with joy.

Edward Hirsch

KRAKOW, 6 A.M.

(for Adam Zagajewski)

I sit in a corner of the town square
and let the ancient city move through me.
I sip a cup of coffee, write a little,
and watch an old woman sweeping the stairs.

Poland is waking up now: blackbirds patrol
the cobblestones, nuns rush by in habits,
and the clock tower strikes six times.
Day breaks into the night's reverie.

The morning is as fresh and clean
as a butcher's apron hanging in a shop.
Now it is pressed and white, but soon
it will be spotted with blood.

Europe is waking up, but America
is going to sleep like a gangly teenager
sprawled out on a comfortable bed.
He has large hands and feet

and his dreams are innocent and bloodthirsty.
I want to throw a blanket over his shoulders
and tuck him in again, like a child,
now that his sleep is no longer untroubled.

I'm alone here in the Old World
where poetry matters, old hatreds seethe,
and history wears a crown of thorns.
Fresh bread wafts from the ovens

and daily life follows its own inexorable
course, like a drunk weaving slowly
across a courtyard, or a Dutch maid
throwing open the heavy shutters.

I suppose there's always a shop-girl
stationed in the doorway, a beggar taking up
his corner post, and newspapers fluttering
from store to store with bad news.

Poetry, too, seeks a place in the world —
feasting on darkness, but needing light,
taking confession, listening for bells,
for the first strains of music in a town square.

Europe is going to work now —
look at those two businessmen hurrying
past the statue of the national bard —
as her younger brother sleeps

on the other side of the ocean,
innocent and violent, dreaming of glory.

Edward Hirsch

THE MINIMALIST MUSEUM

I am driving past our house on Sul Ross
across the street from the minimalist museum.

I am looking up at the second-story window
where I gazed down at the curators

carrying their leather satchels to work
and the schoolchildren gathering on the front lawn.

I spent my forties at that window, stirring milk
into my coffee and brooding about the past,

listening to Satie's experiments and Cage's
dicey music wafting over the temple of modernism.

I chanced a decade at that window, imperious
to the precarious moment, the broken moon-

light flooding over the neighborhood trees,
my wife's moody insomnia, my son's fitful sleep,

and sacrificing another five years, another ten years,
to the minor triumphs, the major failures.

Tony Hoagland

I HAVE NEWS FOR YOU

There are people who do not see a broken playground swing
as a symbol of ruined childhood

and there are people who don't interpret the behavior
of a fly in a motel room as a mocking representation of their
    thought process.

There are people who don't walk past an empty swimming
    pool
and think about past pleasures irrecoverable

and then stand there blocking the sidewalk for other
    pedestrians.
I have read about a town somewhere in California where
    human beings

do not send their tuberous feeder roots
deep into the potting soil of others' emotional lives

as if they were greedy six-year-olds
sucking the last half inch of milkshake up through a noisy
    straw;

and other persons in the Midwest who can kiss without
discussing the imperialist baggage of heterosexuality.

Do you see that creamy, lemon-yellow moon?
There are some people, unlike me and you,

who do not yearn after love or fame or quantities of money as
                            unattainable as that moon;
Thus, they do not later
                have to waste more time
heatedly defaming the object of their former ardor.

Or consequently run and crucify themselves
in some solitary midnight Starbucks Golgotha.

I have news for you:
there are people who get up in the morning and cross a room

and open a window to let the sweet breeze in
and let it touch them all over their faces and bodies.

Tony Hoagland

NATURE

I miss the friendship with the pine tree and the birds
I had when I was ten.
And it has been forever since I pushed my head
under the wild silk skirt of the waterfall.

What I had with them was tender and private.
The lake was practically my girlfriend.
I carried her picture in my front shirt pocket.
Even in my sleep, I heard the sound of water.

The big rock on the shore was the skull of a dead king
whose name we could almost remember.
Under the rooty bank you could dimly see
the bunk beds of the turtles.

Maybe twice had I said a girl's name to myself.
I had not yet had my weird first dream of money.

Nobody I know mentions these things anymore.
It's as if their memories have been seized, erased, and
    relocated
among flow charts and complex dinner party calendars.

Now I want to turn and run back the other way
barefoot into the underbrush,
getting raked by thorns, being slapped in the face by branches.

Down to the muddy bed of the little stream
where my cupped hands make a house, and

I tilt up the roof
to look at the face of the frog.

TEXACO

The nozzle of the gas pump
plunged into the flank of the car
like the curved beak of a predatory bird

looks like it is drinking
or maybe I'm light-headed
from the fumes

or from the slanted light
of Thursday afternoon.
—Still, it is a powerful moment

when I squeeze the trigger of the handle
and feel, beneath the stained cement,
the deep shudder and convulsion

of the gasoline begin
its plunging rush in my direction.
Out of the guts of the earth,

filtered through sand and blood
down the long hose of history
towards the very nipple of this moment:

—the mechanical ticking of the pump,
the sound of my car drinking—
filling my tank with a necessary story

about the road, how we have
to have it to go down;
the whole world construed around

this singular, solitary act
as if I myself had conjured it
from some strange thirst.

Ann Howells

INITIATING MY DAUGHTER

Before your childish body
rounds and softens,
before some smooth-skinned boy
rocks your equanimity,
as night's bright crescent
pierces the eastern sky—
we curl in the porch swing
lap robe tucked about our feet.

Moonflowers twine the railing,
lucent, blue-sheen faces tipped
as I explain little winters
that come before spring, before rebirth:
womb damp, lush with fern—
cushioned bower, life cradle,
where once I cradled you.

Before you outgrow fairytales
still half believed,
before the first blood spills—
I whisper mysteries in your ear,
your eyes wide with wonder
that you, girl-child, are pilgrim
in this ancient rite.

Before you turn in seasons,
before you pull and press the tides,
know that you hold life
behind your flat belly,
clasp miracles in the palm of your hand—
Snow White & Rose Red,
virgin & goddess,
woman.

LONGHORN MOON

You preside over twilight's wash
as it slowly drains after sundown.

You've been there all day along,
but you're hard to spot walking blue sky.

When you stand there like you do right now,
I can imagine those dark eyes watching us closely.

In the morning, when gulls rise up in jubilation
before sunrise, looking for the life of me

like they're trying to pluck Venus from dawn,
you've wandered elsewhere, snorting, pawing

the earth that hides you now.
Waxing in strength, just over the horizon,

you flick your tail at stars as numerous as flies.
The gulls always leave you alone.

Ken Jones

CONCEPTION

Captivate me, swelling sea!
Your buried currents swirl
In descending frenzy
To a pressure point
Where pressure bends defenses
And defensive armor curls.
Once when my life squirmed and slithered
Wiggled and slid
Across the sea bed
I was conceived
In sticky sheets of seaweed
A soft dull head
Burrowed in protective sand
That carpets the crust
That piece on the mantle
That defends the fiery spark
Still bubbling beneath tranquility.
Understanding nothing
But hunger
And the drive for reproduction
Poseidon's slow seduction
Of amino acids and double helix—
Jacob's ladder.

LIMINAL

1.

The only thoughts I ever have
rise between midnight and four
and one of them is a proposal
I never received. As though a life's
map could fall loose like a sheet
shaken from a drawer, I riddle myself
with old words of love, a monolith
made from starfish and sand. You,
yes, I'm still talking to you, never
rendered my cups and bowls, never
drew for me the moment in a home
where two hands reach for the same
crumb. So in the liminal last of this
night, the tenth, I make, humming,
marriage of twittering air: nightbirds
and frogs insist we will be and be.

2.

I was married once, though not
to you, and my oak tree anchored
many mysteries. A linen blouse
on the clothesline slapped your face,
I remember, how you stood there
in a collarless shirt, how I yanked
the flowered drapes shut against
you. The day you came in out
of the rain. There is no wife
like the one I was.

3.

The proposal, my first, would begin
like this: *Crazy Heart, girl, I want
you to understand* and serpentine
bricks studded with Coke bottles

and irises would ever so dully
reflect whatever light was left
as we walked, and every second
the moon (which I bring up only
because it is 91% full and because
the poets say it is dead) bucks up
so you can see my silver toe ring
and the whites of my eyes
and honestly the angling
honeysuckle is pheromone—
I couldn't make that up. No,
I'm sure the way you would pop
some question would involve
Italian cream cake, a public,
colonnades. All the time I would
know something on your mind.
I hug your neck, which hamstrings
the words, keeps them from rising
to air to be chipped into stone.
Your mouth muffled with
my kiss, with sweet vine.

4.
At 3:12 am for all I know
you've gone to bed in another
continent with a harem.
For all I know, you have broken
the seal on a vacuum-packed
love coterie. What we call a day
has never ended for me; tomorrow
matters only as it can be delayed
without sleep. It will come but
in a groggy slush like snow which
I barely remember, though they
tell me it means to be white, like
that great face that through my
windowpane throws gray shadows
to draw plaid stockings on my thighs.

Claire Kageyama-Ramakrishnan

Owens Valley, 1942

For my father and two uncles

Witness the fog and water evaporating from the forbidden
creek, the vapors rising, traveling in tiers over barbed wire up
to the stormclouds' layers of ionizing particles. See how the
day weighs heavily over the Camp, whose inhabitants
anticipate violent showers with the atmosphere's discharge of
electricity, at an hour when the day's light succumbs to the
dark, a darkening which deepens the cleavage of shadow
between the mountains and burst volcanoes. The scene is
worth photographing (if only the cameras hadn't been
confiscated) for the jagged landscape pressing up against the
sky, or for the aspect of horizon resembling stalagmites fitted
to the white-blue stalactites of sky just before the desert's
imminent, unbearable chill sets in, frosting the land and the
adults, and three boys, brothers whose hair curls over their
foreheads, their suspenders glittering with the latest whirl of
sand—mixture of pumice, volcanic ash and glass. They peer
out the doorway of the barracks, hoping they'll see the
shedding, shredded skin of a lizard, the smashed rattler of the
dead snake rolling with the wind hitting the drying, dying
apple tree, in this place called *Home,* called *Camp,* called
Manzanar.

Claire Kageyama-Ramakrishnan

THE MOON AND KAGUYA

It's September 15, 1989.
I'm twenty years old.
My name is Kaguya.

I speak to a flamingo wall.
Autumn lilies smile
in their sleep.
The sky listens.
A wise wind
blows my voice

into the dying apricots.
My hair is dark
as sumi ink.
I let it grow
and trail the back
of my kimono.

Now I change
into a mother dove.
I gather three-hundred twigs
to cup my eggs.
There's a blue jay
on the wire.

I think I'll go
and become a butterfly.
I weave myself
a sugar cocoon
and sleep all year.
A child has licked

my wings.
I can't fly. I'll hide
in a granite pagoda.
The Velveeta moon rises.
A mother opossum is dead.
She lies on the cornstarch hill

curled like a croissant.
Blackbirds have ripped
her belly apart.
Her cubs wait
on the powder trail.

Flies and ants
carry her body in pieces.
They leave behind
her chocolate fur.
I pause
where crows form doves
on the plum horizon.

The oily sea is full
of seaweed lizards.
The sky is empty.
I'm grey as a square
in Escher's drawing.
Yesterday,

you dressed like a yellowtail tuna.
(Kaguya, there isn't such a thing.)
Be quiet moon, I just created it.
(You're only a woman, Kaguya.)
I'm a woman god.
Go away moon—get out of my poem.

(Who will be the moon if I leave?)

I'll make myself the moon.
I rise a new mother.
My children are the platinum stars.
I feed them corn pebbles.
They ask me my name.

I tell them, *I am the pickled moon of November.*
Do not be afraid. The terrible moon
has gone away.

The sun is shining over Europe.
Tonight, I must rise in the East.
I help the wind grind shriveled
sardines into the soil.
We pull back our hair
like dried mushroom stems,
take scissors, cut it off,
until there's nothing left
but a stump of azaleas.

Sharon Klander

GRIEF SONG

for Calvin Ladner, Jr.

i.   *The Old Man*

Even now I can't blame you for the others,
though you were the first, that first disease
you caught and kept like the only way out
of our small family, the wife and two sons

too much. You never asked for forgiveness,
all those mornings we watched your body
break down like a school science project, your face
flush with the day split through kitchen blinds.

Only God knows the strength of a child's faith,
though any father can test it. I once believed
our escapes would save us—you sitting with Mother
and a beer in a house stilted beyond danger,

no matter the kids screaming on the beach
because you couldn't hear us. But now I fear
false hope in those places we leave home for,
in the sunset's slow, elegant pull against water,

that fundamental amber light you'd hold
behind your eyes all the night drive home, all
the long night a plain amber bottle, plain glass.
That soft, lovely roar a boy's voice couldn't penetrate.

ii.   *Brother*

I found you in one corner
on the bed. I wrapped your head
in the sheet.

I've given your clothes, the mattress
to the Goodwill truck, painted your room white,
filled it with books and a desk—

the books to soak up sound.
I'm wrapping your trophies
in paper towels. See how these perfect players

hold their bats high and back
the way Dad taught us. Watch their golden uniforms
falling to flecks in my palms.

iii.   *Mom*

Just as well the old man didn't know.
We'd assumed perpetual health from your starched cap
and stethoscope, the sterile white steps.
We held your hands at his grave: *See what happens*

when you drink. But you did nothing
to start your own slow fall—breast
to bone, legs to rubber-tipped walker, constant
incontinent pain. I prayed for you to live longer

the way children pick the thickest book
for bedtime. I'd beg you for more
as I begged you then, refusing treatment
as if you believed JESUS SAVES, the dog-eared 23rd.

I'd seen the hopeless privacy of disease kept home,
could count days and nights by the hours
someone was still alive upstairs. I want the long,
bleached linoleum halls, Lazarus-level miracles

behind doors, tonsils and tumors dissolved
and wrung out like blood from a shirt.
I want the small glass of water, a scarf-
draped light. All the regular breaths of night.

Jacqueline Kolosov

ORDINARY

Nearing Eighteen Weeks

Moon lights the field—mustard-seed,
hollyhock, summer grass. Within,
the room is candled by a window, needles
and first yarn nesting in a drawer.
                    Across the threshold,
into a night small enough to hold both of us,
and our daughter—*she's with us always now*—
the dogs following.

Daily, we cross the meadow, waiting
for the Texas sun to swallow the horizon.
Through August's ochres, umbers,
and the occasional flash of spearmint,
heat lingering. Drift of feedlot,
cottonseed.
                    Rambles lead us
back to a garden heavy with tomatoes
and the scent of thyme. The roses'
leaves crumble between our fingertips.
Still, every week puts forth a new bloom.
                    Hands along my belly,
there, too, ripening—*she's with us always
now*—I write to her with my palms,
letters bidden not by language,
but by the feel of lambs' ear, rich soil.

On the doorstep, the neighbor's
white cat—one blue eye, the other gold—
and in the neighbor's garden, sun-
flowers sprung from the birdfeeder's leavings.

Jacqueline Kolosov

POISED

At the back gate, a covey
of inca doves, and the courteous dog,
prick ears cocked, poised for a visitor.

This morning feels gentle
as the hand that cups the fallen fledgling,
as the kiss that calms the startled child.

Laddered between *anything is possible*
and *the unforeseen*, patience
is the cardinal seen through deep snow.

Or perhaps, it is the dark-voiced
pony swishing its tail in a silent pasture.
At its feet, a thousand white flowers
await their chance to bloom.

And within my womb, you, too, are waiting.
Not quite January, and already
I am twining spring's leaf-flocked
blossoms through your hair.

Judith Kroll

The Summer after the Storm

Sitting in a patch of monsoon sunlight,
we catch it while we can.

Meeting in the space between our houses,
myself and my neighbor
who left her college just near the end,
agreed to the match her parents arranged,
got married, and had two sons.

We're warming our hands on glasses of hot spiced tea,
still in the clothes we slept in last night.

Beside us, flowers in rusty old tins.
I point to one: "What do you call that here?"

"Dancing Lady," my neighbor says.

"*We* call it Bleeding Heart."

We look at each other and burst out laughing,
laughing and laughing like kids
about to be scolded for laughing so much,
but we can't stop:

my neighbor who cooks and cleans all day,
with always someone to make her dance
to the tunes they play: husband,
in-laws, sons—she is
the dancing lady

while I
have none of that,

I who dance to my books, my little computer,
my reams of American paper,

I am the bleeding heart
from the bleeding empire

and it fits that this morning another
Indian friend
phones me and says: I have an insight
into your president.
Mr. Bush is a very quiet man.

"I told you I don't like him," I reply,
as if that answers something—
as it doesn't and it does

and my friend says
(the story of my life)
Maybe you should.

Laurie Clements Lambeth

WRONG TURN NEAR PECOS

I don't know where I am.
The road's inhabitants don't know
what I am. Tentative, reserved,

they hop onto asphalt, until all
the jackrabbits, thirty-one, freeze,
held by high beams. The asphalt breaks

behind them into grass. Fawn gray, or dirt
brown I'd call them, long freakish ears and huge
unfolded tails. They're poised as if

interrupted in mid-thought, gazing
at the still car, at me. These creatures remind
me of my own quiet childhood, the china

animals I played with, gently, their shoe-
box home marked "fragile." Fuzz
on porcelain, thin, gray, the same

color as these rabbits, deer, brush.
The pupils of their brown glass eyes seemed real
until now, when I see these rabbits' eyes

redden, like glass in a kiln. But
these things without motion are living,
posed, proving I cannot drive an inch

farther. Their paws block the road. I pause,
then cut the wheel left to back down
the way I came. But the animals line up

close to the road, so I turn right. Under
my right rear tire I hear something.
I can't tell whether it's china or bone.

Erica Lehrer

1554.8

If you didn't live one thousand five hundred
fifty-four point eight miles away, I would bake a bread
of the richest most delicious pumpernickel, sweetened
with honey, in the breadmaker I considered buying —
but didn't, having realized, as I stood conversing
with the aproned salesman with thinning hair,
that I didn't have anyone to bake for, at least
no one within driving distance — although, certainly,
the distance between us is drivable if I spent
several days behind the wheel of a car, crossing
Texas, New Mexico, Arizona and most of California.

Sometime after sunrise, I'd leave the bread — so fragrant! —
on your doorstep, wrapped in a blue cloth napkin
in a wicker basket filled with jams and a carafe
of chilled juice squeezed from oranges plucked
from a tree in my backyard — if I had an orange tree.
Then, enjoying the morning birdsong, I'd linger
on your top step. Still dawdling, I'd look up, marveling
that the trees lining your street form a green canopy,
their outstretched branches touching overhead; and that,
for those trees, planted as saplings a century ago,
the distance they've traveled through time and space to reach
each other in many ways exceeds the one thousand five hundred
fifty-four point eight miles I would travel, across
state lines, mountains, ravines and deserts,
to your door.

A DREAM

No matter how I try I can't
flush her down. Or rather
she won't *stay* down. Her long pale
body disappears for a moment,

and then I lift the lid, and
like a person-shaped circus balloon
she pops up, head in bowl, toes
pointed, and bobs there.

I can't believe it. People are coming—
I hear their footsteps and
laughter—she has to go. I lift her out
for what I hope is the last time,

and she is as light as a feather, a thing
made of light, a kind of persistent
life-sized ghost, except that now
she's headless. Once again

I shove her down the hole,
flush, wash my hands, close the door
behind me, and try to pretend
I don't care what's next

as the first guests arrive.

Rich Levy

EMERGENCIES

At the emergency room in the children's
hospital, you want someone to do something

about the dog bite on your teenage daughter's leg,
which has grown hard and dark, and hurts.

In the next bed, a childlike mother holds
her gasping infant boy in her arms and coos, *Ay ay ay-ay,*

while the father cups the child's head
in his hand. You can tell they can't afford this,

but they will wait and wait. Minutes later, a nurse
takes his temperature, the infant screams,

and in a voice reserved for the "foreign" and dim,
the nurse reports that the fever, 105, has

not declined. Down the hall, a child moans,
another shouts, "Ma," and you've gotten almost

nowhere in your catalogs, while your daughter
reads *Us* and *Star*, sucks on her cell phone

antenna, and howls, "Girl," when her
glum friend arrives. And then, as you do,

you imagine it all going wrong, the bite
launching an infection that kills her, and you,

bereaved father, gazing at the grave. Or perhaps
you bolt to Mexico or France, smitten

by a scenic grief. Then all at once you're
collecting your things, the doctor's shaking

your hand, embolism gone, daughter's leg
taped, and what spooked you on a Sunday night

is reduced, hours later, to an incision,
prescription, and shot. The girls shriek

at someone's dress or shoes in yet another
scene from the movie of their lives

as they hobble out, and you nod
to the couple, leaning over their splayed

son and half-dead themselves, who stare
like cattle behind a fence

beginning to suspect something.

Michael Lieberman

GRATITUDE

I burned the crocuses when they danced naked in gray New
     Haven—
and after in Pittsburgh and St. Louis. I sat next to no one,
hoarded the oysterettes at my kitchen table in the tired light.
Only once or twice have I allowed myself to teem beyond the
     ordinary.
And now in this jowled abundance I stumble and dance.
Even if the gloom remain, I am glad for any sun that should
     rise—
pushed up by her own design or otherwise.
I cling to the tiny strawberries in the wild meadows of certain
     hearts.
I am the heartworm of those hearts, no more, and I am
     grateful.

Michael Lieberman

SEPTEMBER 11, 2001

1. Kyrie

This is the same porch I sat on reading Mihail Sebastian,
    where I drank the same double strength coffee and
    brooded,
the same place where I wondered about apologists for evil and
    those who brook no apology for evil,
where today I am confronting secrets, meanings I imagine—a
    dog circling before the hearth or lifting its leg to a tree, acts
    that are not predestined but inevitable,
necessary for the business of being a dog, how our behavior is
    nourished by the cells we nourish, and the flowers on
    every stem are both different and the same.
For some events awkward anapests pretend root causes, yet
    what seems encrypted in culture resides a layer down.
So when I look at the encumbering dactyls of the past that
    clasp us, I move to the realm of spiders and insects, how
    they engulf or burrow into their mates and prey—
as if Fabre, not Clausowitz explained Bunker Hill and Dien
    Bien Phu, as if the how-to of solitary wasps is our guide.
The boiler-plate evil of the twentieth century remains with us,
    not a repeat of the past, but a portrayal of the tumbling
    shards of our neural circuits.

God is relative and a relative, holding forth at the podium on
    sundry items—the shrink-wrapped odds and ends of our
    lives—
all talk is sundry and relative. My God does not trash, He's
    not a gossip, but when He represents His views, there's no
    correspondence,
nothing lingers but indefinable essences that find no place in
    words—the smell of basil and the smell of shit.
When I read of Mihail Sebastian reproving the evil -escu's of
    his world and how dactylic Homer left Achilles dead, I
    cannot not grasp the meaning or rely on grief and pity.

The Iron Guard in Romania is a play with too may characters,
and our legacy of Troy remains small towns, football
teams and condoms.

Our world is a map without coordinates, ditto our
ministrations to the Lord. What are good works good for?
We cannot apply a yardstick to a song.

Try to imagine a croissant without olfaction, a club without
prehension, chess without cognition. Try to imagine God
Almighty.

The subbasement of the Towers is amines and serotonin,
receptors and evolution, developmental biology and
animal behavior.

I long for relativism that is relevant. Whether there is one God
or not I do not know, but there are many prophets—
Darwin, Lorenz, Tinbergen, Von Frisch, E.O. Wilson,
others.

In Provence Van Gogh and Gauguin grappled to find a way in
by looking out. For Vincent the merge of sun and wheat
and sky yielded the essential truth of chartreuse, a gaudy
remnant that Gauguin refused in his own distortions, the
two of them struggling in Arles, working in Vincent's
yellow house.

And Others. Pasteur in Paris dissected the inner logic of
chirality in lactic acid crystals and Emil Fischer concurred,
Mahler and Bruckner embraced music to expel their
demons, Freud and Jung like two hemispheres of thought
forced us bolt-upright in the night,

Pairs of fraternal twins, towering above their peers divergent
and convergent, resistant to implosion, fanatic and
committed.

2. Gloria

Dear Wystan Hugh,
I wish I had your view
(or what was thought your view)
of love and death.

What's up my sorcerer sleeve
is that there's no reprieve.
Nothing ends with whimper or sigh—
we won't love one another, but die.

Each reads his sacred text,
no better than the next,
to secure a hearth and home,
permission for a bomb.
We're right, of course we're right
except when we are wrong.
Our offenses are less egregious
simply because we're religious,
our humanists agree—
they're us without a trinity.

3. Credo

When it comes to rubble and loss,
I believe in nostalgia—speak-easys
and gangsters with tommy guns,
the rags-to-riches ketch that spares us.
What obscures skewers—
the pipes of Hibernians
marching on St. Patrick's Day
mean homage and resolve.
No script or text takes precedence,
no pretext can prevail—
pre-text impulses flood our every action.
Impulse is what gives impulse traction.

Our inheritance is neurons.
Being well connected means our axons.
Memory is triplet snags of DNA
that catch our decency and dreams

as schemes for tomorrow and today.
We struggle with these, against these,
improvident beings whose search
for the light consists only of sight.
Our retinas and cortical patterns
capture the surface of what happens—
spelling bees, saints and slatterns,
Jihad, Koran, and Talibans—
valued by mindless acts of mind.

We live with loss and reprisal
turning over in our minds,
a zero-sum game, a sudden-death match
with every knight and pawn both black and white.
From every shires ende
to happenstance we *wende*.
No contortion helps us slip our bind.
No destiny is manifest,
our only hope is kindness met in kind.

Thad Logan

On the Road to San Antonio

Vertical bolts of lightning rip the sky up ahead,
and an ugly, cigar-shaped cloud rolls right down I-10;
there's the usual afternoon glare, but it's weird
in the distance, too dark for five o'clock; it's OK, though,
I'm on the phone, getting past construction, past the traffic,
almost to Katy before it lightens up, and by then the storm's
    veered
north, thundering its way to Tomball and points east;
I'm in the clear, except for some rain, rain that should stop,
soon, because the sun's come out, rain that should let up
    pretty quick—
but doesn't; the sun keeps getting lower till its just about level
with my eyeballs, and it's raining harder all the time,
so hard I can't quite feel the road, and something's happening
on the windshield: the raindrops burst against it, reflecting
    light;
rain's hitting the glass like little balls of mercury we played
    with
out of broken thermometers, in the days when everyone in
    America
was too young to know any better, and if I could see past that,
which I can't, much, I'd see that the cars up ahead seem to be
    traveling
in strange cocoons of darkness, made up I guess of some
    unholy mess
of steam and exhaust and oily water thrown upward from the
    road:
I can just make out their red lights in the filthy air; meanwhile
    the sun
has decided to see how close it can get to becoming a
    supernova
before it sets, and it's as though I'm squinting into fire,
and all the time the rain comes down so hard I can't see to
    drive,

but I can't stop, because I can't see to stop either,
and I'm sliding down the road amazed to be alive,
when finally we get a break, and the rain slows, and the sun
     goes
below the horizon, and it's just another Friday on the freeway
in the violent state where I was born, on a violent planet
skidding around a star in the middle of nowhere.

THE MOST BEAUTIFUL WORDS

In English, according to Henry James
are *summer afternoon*.
Until I came to this wide porch,
I didn't get it. Now I do.

The dogs sleep like babies
flat out in the sunshine.
Butterflies drift in and out of flowers.
Across the creek, at the edge of the woods,
black walnuts, three slim sisters
wave many-fingered light-green hands.
Now the maples answer
in a rush of whispers, and the willow
stirs like water in the wind.

It's not quite sleep that comes to me
in the wicker in the shade.
It isn't sleep that moves across the hillside,
with footsteps cool and bright, and yet
I'm slowed and half undone by bliss.

From here, I can't quite follow
the voices on the news:
from this distance words wash out.
Even "innocent." Even "suffering."

Robert Lunday

HANDS

(excerpts from a book-length hybrid poem)

After she had succeeded in resealing the box,
Pandora took a moment to marvel
        at the living movie of release—

        ribbons of pestilence and rape,
        earth-trembling, madness, kwashiorkor,
        hurricanes, drowning—

        all winding and spreading,
but so alive with color and motion
for a moment, she simply had to watch;

        then in horror at her fascination,
shut the lid—

        and marveled at the box itself,
        its craftsmanship,
        its beauty and lightness;

hope alone remained inside,

        scintillated,
        weightless;

were she to open it again
        wouldn't the box,
        the beautiful box,
be empty?

———————

        With an arrow
Cupid cut his mother's nails
        as she slept;

the parings fell into the Indus, sank to the bottom, becoming
    jewels —

      onyxes, black and white,

      day and night,

      phase-states,

         competing absolutes —

      or fell into a lover's phrases, pearled commas:
shimmering waste, as each superlative

      gives way to an ascendant praise.

**An ornithologist brought his equipment to the forests of the
    lyrebird**; he set up his recording devices and listened.

Instead of the mimicking bird, he heard the Doppler effect of a
    passing airplane, the teeth of a saw, the shouts of workmen
    who were building a road not far off, but weren't there at
    the time.

He heard an anthill; he heard eyelashes and his own ear.

He recorded everything, but he didn't catch the lyrebird.

Then, one day, he did come upon the lyrebird, barking like a
    dog on its mound. He chased it down a hill to a clearing
    near the mouth of an abandoned mine.

There, he found many more lyrebirds, roosting, flying about,
    as if they were themselves all of creation. The
    ornithologist recorded it all, until he could hold no more;
    he was overstuffed with the mockery, he was beginning to
    feel indistinguishable from it.

Then he played the tape back. The lyrebirds seemed offended,
    either at themselves, or at the scientist, and flew off in one
    great concert of departure. Instead of the beating of wings,

the man heard something like applause—loud, watery
applause, even after the birds had disappeared.

Someone asks, of the severed head,
lying there in the basket beneath the shining fallen blade,
if it did not remain aware for several seconds?—

long enough to hear this question, and judge it meaningless?

When I skydived for the first time,
I was keenly aware of the whiteness of the air;

my experience completely encircled me,
I was stretched out like a giant hand,
I was aware of nothing but the sky,
there was no up or down, no left or right,

and the earth, which I knew was beneath me,
seemed sunk below its own horizon;

I could see, to put it differently,
but my seeing stopped at the eyes;

my eyes were like fingertips,
and all I knew was

        I was there,

        and falling;

if there was a ladder,
my hands must have been the rungs.

Peggy Zuleika Lynch

DEMAND AT LA CLOSERIES DES LILAS

Hot, hot, hot
this steamy evening,
sitting here with Hemmingway's ghost
mirroring our minds,
torturing our desires,
grotesquely dominating
our posture,
clawing our consciousness
like a gargoyle guarding
Notre Dame de Paris.

Cynthia Macdonald

AND CAUSE HIS COUNTENANCE TO SHINE UPON YOU:
CORPUS CHRISTI, TEXAS

The rabbi and his wife live in the body of Christ.
They break bread in it and drink dark, red Mogen David
To break the Yom Kippur fast. The ribs of the city
Rise around them, and its long watery arms and legs
Embrace them as the belt of the causeway lights up at dusk,
Securing the sky's dark fabric around the heart of the town,
Covering its pubis, South Bluff Park, which shelters
The strolling Rabbi and his wife from the Gulf Coast's sexual heat.
The city's beard, seaweed studded with shrimp, oysters and
     crayfish,
Hangs from the face of the sea with its changeable weathers—
Tense as religion or grammar, calm as beatitude or the full moon,
Joyous as a dance in the shtetl or on Fat Tuesday, as the mouth's
First savor of Aunt Martha's matzoh balls, swimming
In a richer salty broth. The eyes of Christ span the gulf of
Time looking back at himself, just after B.C., when he sat
At the long table, dividing the Passover matzoh. There was no
Poland yet so the matzoh was still a wafer, flat as the world.

The Rabbi prepares for Yom Kippur. His best friend is
The Methodist minister. Perhaps here in Corpus Christi—the
     body
Of Christ—there will be no pogroms. My Great-grandfather
     Kiam—
Loch Chaim—kissed the ground when he landed in New
     Orleans,
Kissed the body of American earth, thanked God, and set off
For the middle of Texas where a town that no longer exists
Was named after him. He celebrated Passover
Outside in the American desert of Amarillo, eating fried
Pinto beans, chili peppers and a boiled egg, which was
What there was. My mother showed me Kiam, Texas

In the 1934 Rand McNally Atlas while my sister tried
To straighten her crossed eyes by exercising them with
The stereopticon. Then we had Sunday breakfast, always
Bacon, eggs, and popovers. My grandfather's wife, Fanny
     Tim,

A New Yorker, a German Jew, stuck a hat pin in her
Fine straw hat or her winter felt with its grosgrain ribbon
And rosette or flowers or cherries, and left to hear
John Haynes Holmes preach at the Congregational Church.

At night, the rigs burn their anointing oils to provide a halo of
     light
For the head of Christ. The rabbi dives into the black water,
With its rainbow patina, swimming laps over the Day of
     Atonement,
Struggling, like all Jews, to know the place where he lives.

Cynthia Macdonald

TWO BROTHERS IN A FIELD OF ABSENCE

Because as they cut it was that special green, they decided
To make a woman of the fresh hay. They wished to lie in
    green, to wrap
Themselves in it, light but not pale, silvered but not grey,
Green and ample, big enough so both of them could shelter
    together
In any of her crevices, the armpit, the join
Of hip and groin. They—who knew what there was to know
    about baling
The modern way with hay so you rolled it up like a carpet,
Rather than those loose stacks—they packed the green body
    tight
So she wouldn't fray. Each day they moulted her to keep her
Green and soft. Only her hair was allowed to ripen into
    yellow tousle.

The next weeks whenever they stopped cutting they lay with her.
She was always there, waiting, reliable, their green woman.
She gathered them in, yes she did,
Into the folds of herself, like the mother they hadn't had.
Like the women they had had, only more pliant, more graceful,
Welcoming in a way you never just found.
They not only had the awe of taking her,
But the awe of having made her. They drank beer
Leaning against the pillow of her belly
And one would tell the other, "Like two Adams creating,"
And they marveled as they placed
The cans at her ankles, at her neck, at her wrists so she
Glittered gold and silver. They adorned what they'd made.
After harrowing they'd come to her, drawing
The fountains of the plains, the long line
Of irrigating spray and moisten her up,

And lean against her tight, green thighs to watch buzzards
Circle black against the pink stain of the sunset.

What time she began to smolder they never knew—
Sometime between night when they'd left her
And evening when they returned. Wet, green hay
Can go a long time smoldering before you notice. It has a way
Of catching itself, of asserting that
There is no dominion over it but the air. And it flares
    suddenly
Like a red head losing her temper, and allows its long bright
    hair
To tangle in the air, letting you know again
That what shelters you can turn incendiary in a flash.
And then there is only the space of what has been,
An absence in the field, memory in the shape of a woman.

BING CHERRIES, PURPLE PLUMS

Anatomy. Pathology.
This building reeks of death.
Long past the sudden lust for breath,
the astonished grunt, they lie.
A hand, a foot, an eye
glimmering in its clever fringe of lash.

The dark comes down so early now.
I need your arms, sure and alive.
Your mouth, what it must have.
That twisting pinch of urgency
against my brow.

Summer will come, oh, say it will.
Smelling of Sea and Ski.
Rickety stands beside the roads.
Bing cherries, grapes
and those dark fleshy plums.
All the tight-skinned fruit
that bursts and runs.
Car radios, sun
and Queen Anne's lace
and God, we will forget this basement place.

Formaldehyde. Formaldehyde.
These lungs devoid of breath.
Anatomy. Pathology.
Winter stinks of death.

John R. Milkereit

REMINISCING ABOUT MATCHSTICKS

Remember the best ones from nine-thousand years ago?
We rubbed two together with our hands
causing a resistance between two bodies
we later learned was friction, and a fire
ensued inside that cave, our cores warmed,
we roasted what I killed, we survived the winters
somehow.

Where have the 1800s gone? We made small strips
of wood and paper tipped with a combustible material.
We lived in France for a while and upgraded to phosphorus.
Later, we moved to America and found twelve in a book.
We struck them using the tips of our fingers against a narrow
oxidizing landing strip that I will never forget.

Have you forgotten what happened last summer?
The generic jacketed ones had camped in an amber
rust candle plate cussing and swapping stories about nothing.
They punched plumeria candles across the walnut
grains of our Queen Anne table. They avoided fallen rose
petals, salt granulars, and sudden plateaus of newspapers.
They even yanked a wagon of incense from Bangalore.

Yesterday they rode from San Antonio in a box
labeled *Little Rhein Steak House,*
Nick's Fishmarket swam downstream from Chicago
and rendezvoused with *The Daily Grind* —
a local guide for the artic journey across the porcelain
tundra of our bathroom. They climbed the toilet basin towing
a candle layered in gardenia, seminole rain, and eggplant.
Certainly, it was an adventurous time to be alive, or at least cold.

Today, I am thinking about the extinguished ones of the past,
their brief little lives caused us to survive, and rescued us
from the jaws of boredom. I am even thinking about the future—
we could fly them to another planet, a place we can only guess,
start over again, and tell stories around a campfire,
stories we can only imagine.

Laura Elizabeth Miller

SHE OPENED HER MOUTH LIKE A GREAT FISH

And swallowed the book. Down it fell through salt and glass stars, past the spikes and spires of her heart's metropolis. It shook the frozen sidewalk when it struck. Her heart blinked a snow-crusted eye. In their rush, people tripped and stumbled over the book, kicking it into an alley, where it fell open and burst into flame. Dense smoke stretched black branches toward the roofs and dug roots through the pavement. And when the ancient keeper of the heart climbed the subterranean stair to the street, she reached up for a little snow from a low branch to cool her brow, and drew back a handful of blossoms.

DESCENT; A PROGRESS NOTE

We called them
            progress notes not
counseling session summaries.

Progress indicated
      a movement forward
          a   progression

toward healing, that money was
          being used wisely,

that wounds were sealing,
that our words were
          softening scars
into flat white lines.

Each note began the same:
sex, age and lineage.

Along the border
      it meant rarely
changing *of Mexican descent*
          meaning Hispanic
      on monthly reports.

Descent: a fall,
as in sometimes misspelled or
      altered to decent
      the act of
      appearing respectable
      and moral,

meaning not
wearing a tight skirt,
not being drunk or
    not appearing
        gay.

Decent will not lead to rape.
    Decent is a hand
against a tidal wave
        water
        has power over bodies.

I look into water pooled
        in my palm
words appear inversed
I provide translation
            add three letters
channel my mother's voice
        no seas indecente.

    Or dissent. To rebel
to not do
    as I was told
        confined to edges
    of progress notes.

        I'd allow words
to hang over the side.
    An act of dissent to misspell
the word descent.

    It wasn't decent of me
        to get back at the ED
in this way when she wrote me
        up for wearing a shirt deemed indecent.

Flippant is the word
     she used not
defiant, not with fist raised
but with hair tossed over shoulder.

     Flippant, my voice in ashes
on my tongue.
Not fire.

With each note, a new
     spelling descended
                    one from the next
               until I couldn't find my way
back to the correct word.
Until I wouldn't allow myself
     to find the exact word. In-
decent to believe
I could even know the language needed.
     To believe I could posses
a complete understanding of what
               had happened to each client.
               Notes in monotony desen-
          sitize, templates give sessions form.

Words descended down
margins.

I held meaning
at the edge of understanding.

Jack Myers

TAKING THE CHILDREN AWAY

They will pack the sky blue car
with blankets and pillows
and puzzles and snacks,
enough to end a life,
and the last thing I will see
will be the stuffed animals
pressed against the window,
like a happy ending in a Muppet movie,
tiny hands like wings
waving goodbye, little voices
trailing out the sides like streamers.

I will stand there
in the suicidal, accelerating, horizontal draft
of the car longer than is natural,
feeling liberated,
like a bombed-out town,
as the sad blue car dwindles and darkens
and inhales itself,
and I enter the house,
turn off the lights,
sit in foreclosure,
watching the twinkling half-life
of fallout begin floating down the years,
scattered toys appearing one by one
the way the first evening stars
look left behind.

This must be the missing that begins
inside the waiting for something larger
to take over, the being over to be over
that feels like the cobalt hand of air
I think my soul must be. I am afraid

that it will take a breath and then another
and another, like steps, until I begin to glow
like the small dull bulb inside a doorbell
as the evening sun slowly, simply disappears.

Jack Myers

TRAINING HORSES

> *You are alone with Alone,*
> *and it's his move.*
> —*Robert Penn Warren*

Once in a while, if I lie still and am quiet,
I can still feel the trembling, prehistoric,
galactic static between stations
I used to listen to for patterns as a kid.

Marci whispered "Make friends with it,"
and blew into her stallion's nose who closed his eyes,
gathered himself, shivered, and suddenly quieted.

The stable was dark and rich and sweet and moist, and the
    darkness
seemed to deepen with the breathing of her exquisite horses
as she explained how her best thoroughbred was "broke to
    death,"
had lost his edge though he still trembled and reared and
    shied away
and battered his stall and roared and gnawed on wood so
    addictively
he would no longer stop to eat.

I couldn't read his huge brown eyes
that stretched whatever he saw across them,
but merely by the pressing of my knees or the clicking of my
    tongue,
I commanded his massive heart
to take the most delicate steps.
Later that night we made love and lost ourselves a bit,
and Marci slept, and I stared into the fire, bemused,
a little buzzed, my divorce about final, and listened hard

to the night that arced like a test pattern
over the little ranch and us,
but could make no sense of the quiet.

I thought it's useless to marry again and again
though nothing I knew could stop me.
Eventually, the thought of him going crazy out there
alone in the dark was enough for her to put him down.
That night I went out back to the pitch black square
where he had been kept, so I could see his stall for myself.

Naomi Shihab Nye

FOR MOHAMMED ZEID OF GAZA, AGE 15

There is no *stray* bullet, sirs.
No bullet like a worried cat
crouching under a bush,
no half-hairless puppy bullet
dodging midnight streets.
The bullet could not be a pecan
plunking the tin roof,
not hardly, no fluff of pollen
on October's breath,
no humble pebble at our feet.

So don't gentle it, please.

We live among stray thoughts,
tasks abandoned midstream.
Our fickle hearts are fat
with stray devotions, we feel at home
among bits and pieces,
all the wandering ways of words.

But this bullet had no innocence, did not
wish anyone well, you can't tell us otherwise
by naming it mildly, this bullet was never the friend
of life, should not be granted immunity
by soft saying—friendly fire, straying death-eye,
why have we given the wrong weight to what we do?

Mohammed, Mohammed, deserves the truth.
This bullet had no secret happy hopes,
it was not singing to itself with eyes closed
under the bridge.

THE SMALL VASES FROM HEBRON

Tip their mouths open to the sky.
Turquoise, amber,
the deep green with fluted handle,
pitcher the size of two thumbs,
tiny lip and graceful waist.

Here we place the smallest flower
which could have lived invisibly
in loose soil beside the road,
sprig of succulent rosemary,
bowing mint.

They grow deeper in the center of the table.

Here we entrust the small life,
thread, fragment, breath.
And it bends. It waits all day.
As the bread cools and the children
open their gray copybooks
to shape the letter that looks like
a chimney rising out of a house.

And what do the headlines say?

Nothing of the smaller petal
perfectly arranged inside the larger petal
or the way tinted glass filters light.
Men and boys, praying when they died,
fall out of their skins.
The whole alphabet of living,
heads and tails of words,
sentences, the way they said,
"Ya'Allah!" when astonished,

or "ya'ami" for "I mean" —
a crushed glass under the feet
still shines.
But the child of Hebron sleeps
with the thud of her brothers falling
and the long sorrow of the color red.

Monica Teresa Ortiz

DENTIST APPOINTMENT

To speak the sort of English lingualized
by a girl from Texas, I hardly open my mouth,
never lick my consonants, so every sentence spoken
authors
some kind of wonderful dedication
to swallowing as many letters
in one conversation as possible.
I'm not sure where they go—the missing letters that is.
Maybe they end up in Tulsa or Clovis.
I think I talk pretty good, even without those lost letters.
Spanish is another matter. I board a Greyhound bus
at the station on Santa Fe Street in El Paso,
bound for Hereford, the closest stop
to where my parents live. I can't speak a spic
of Spanish and the bus is full of Mexicans and
Chicanos and a few Americans so I sit
by and by a window and wait, watching
blur of buildings pass by and erratic Volkswagens and
Ford Fiestas with Chihuahua license plates zing
alongside the bus, to see if I can make it
without uttering a single noise.
All my noises occur in English
I'm often told it's irresponsible
and disgraceful behavior not to know my mother
tongue, the very idiom exchanged over the carving of the turkey
     and
spoonfuls of sopita during Thanksgiving
supper in my house. I'm unable to articulate
blessed open awed movement of a voice praying
the rosary with the Virgen Santa.
Spanish speakers hemorrhage words.
I shark them. I'm kind of cheap.
Don't spend a cent on the language and pocket the pennies

of my alphabet. A blind woman next to me
reaches out and says,
me hace el favor de avisarme cuando lleguemos a Las Cruces.[1]
I shortchange her
pretend I'm deaf
and can't hear a thing.

[1] Not speaking Spanish does not qualify me for a handicap parking
   sticker.

ENLISTMENT PAPERS

I tried to be a Zapatista once
purchased a black ski mask at Wal-Mart
off I-35 jerked mask taut over my head
cranked up Bob Dylan read
Marx in bed smoked
a cigarette joined
MECHA drank coffee at the Cactus
where Janis razor-rimmed blues passed out
orange flyers on the West Mall brandished
my placard in front of the capital building flipped
down Everclear shots and scrawled plans on paper
napkins to
take back Chiapas
saved paychecks to enlist
in the movement the Indigenous needed me
to free them

Mom asked me, *why are you going to Mexico?*
you don't even know who Zapata is

I did know
from an old black and white
postcard tacked on my bedroom wall
bought for $2 at a flea market in San Antonio
Zapata's poised as if He-man Master of the Universe
[my heroes come in brown]
I looked at his black eyes gleaming
like pools of viscous tar
and read his words written
underneath his black boots
in big black letters:
I'd rather die on my feet than live
on my knees

I wanted to live like that die
like that
for a cause for a
revolution for a
movement I wanted to be
a martyr to believe
in something
my mom said *sainthood*
won't come from saving Chiapas
she said *heroes never live long enough*
to enjoy their legacy and do you
really want to get killed before 19?
if so she would rather
me join the Army or the Marines
at least my family gets money for that

my black mask packed in a box I
spent the money on a trip to Monterrey
to paint a schoolhouse and hand out
soup cans to homeless I
mailed five bucks a month
to a kid in Mexico City and
read Steinbeck's *Zapata* instead

Mary Gomez Parham

LISTENING TO ST. THERESA

Today I snipped threads from the bathroom
rug and then I bathed the dog;

then I turned a hem on my husband's pants
and after that I put some beans on to stew.

I tried to write a poem
but could find nothing to say.

Then I remembered St. Theresa
said *Dios está en las ollas.*

If he is, if God really is crouched
squirming inside a 3-quart pot under my sink,

why couldn't there be poetry inside my vacuum
cleaner's dirty bag?

Maybe I let it go wasted
down the drain when I bathe the dog

and should see the drowning fleas
as Dante's dead or Bosch's damned.

I'd write more poems if I looked
closer: I might find

lovers entangled in the lint
on a rug or see pinto beans'

brown and white as, say, a struggle
between Darkness and Light.

As I watched them boil in salt and water,
poetic Truth would rise in the steam

and I'd ladle out a perfect sonnet into a white bowl.

Dave Parsons

AUSTIN RELATIVITY

for Fred Hanna, Eddie Peterson, Bobby Jones
and my many other fellow Lifeguards of the Sixties.

The old flagship Night Hawk Restaurant sits at a memory axis—
just over the Colorado River Bridge, where Riverside Drive
    crosses

South Congress running east toward the Bergstrom Air Force
    Base;
where, at the guarded entrance the large painted water tank
    spouted

PEACE IS OUR PROFESSION, the home of Dr. Strangelove's
bombers of the sixties; and later, those chillingly beautiful
    aquiline

Phantom jets streaking over the emerald hill country rolls
in the seventies and eighties; this same road ran west past the
    lazy

hills of Barton Springs, where those stunningly free living
    hippie
sprites would play and lay topless, sprawled across the lush

north green banks . . . across from the icy blue pumping
    methodical
flow of the springs that fronted my guard stand, appearing

at times as bodies strewn like casualties of some insidious sun
bomb, as I sweltered in baby oil mixed with the bold blood

of iodine, squinting over small patches of zinc oxide, musing
to the radio sounds of the Stones, Dylan, the many varied

voices that pumped with steely laced drum beats a music
into the heart of our turbulent days, instilling an urgent urge

to physically act—to escape from the stagnant pools of our
    youth,
to dive in to the current of whitewater energy of the times,
    swim

that dark and intoxicatingly mystery, that dangerous rushing,
    rushing—

Dave Parsons

ORANGE COUNTY APRIL 29, 2005

It is Friday and though I am over a thousand miles away,
I can see you clearly in the east Texas morning
rolling away from my vacant side of the bed
to your feet, as you are compelled
to do every early morning, moving
militarily through the mechanics — creating
another day: the first call of the toilet,
shuffling to the kitchen, water for the kettle,
the daily dolling out of the medicine
to the white counter top, the orbiting shuttle
to our sleepy daughter's bedside
for the exchange of her pills for the small dog
curled resistantly warm under their covers —

        And there you are . . . there between the oak tree
and the row of dogwoods doing dog duty on your birthday —
what are you thinking today?   If I were there, with you
I would not know — behind the physical — the mundane
there is the wonder, the mysterious and unique impulse
that resides in the essence of you — the creation of stunning art
out of the dark world of your haunting subconscious —
I have rarely been able to guess those memories, those
    thoughts —
even if I were on that common quay — my face inches
from yours, falling, plummeting dizzily into the auburn
framed countenance of your glowing presence — tripping
into the folds of your graceful familiar form, fixed
in wonder on that onyx centering in the greyhound blue eyes,
where that ineffable chalcedonic entity resides and in some
oblique way, *takes dominion of all that surrounds.*

Emmy Pérez

IT'S POURING

It's pouring boys racing past lowered red truck stopped in hollywood flitter. She said it's pouring conjunto. He said it's pouring gals with tight jeans lit up with wow pow lights. It's pouring morning in cerveza bottles, cucarachas walking upright on walls. Security in golf cart rounds checking it all out. It's pouring young men grabbing gals for public kisses. The smell of lemongrass and urine pouring from stadium lights. It's pouring green parakeets squawking in between tall-glass-of-water mesquites, between telephone wires dangling the bluest notes. It's pouring squabbling over grammar and patrol zones—oops, the nose lit up red when metal tweezers dipped in. It's pouring dropping in unannounced without sotol or ether. It's pouring conspiracy theories—thunder breaking beak calls & two second respites from hot weather.

Emmy Pérez

MIDNIGHT ROOSTER SONG

Chemicals in my lull trigger the roosters' fractured succession
of throats and songs after the midnight procession. Let us peel
off lingerie in sewer air.

I lapped up my clichés in Walmart's parking lot: vatos gliding
by in low-riders, staring me down, mistaking my thirst for
trouble, not lust. I'm home.

Sing me a narcocorrido. Sing me geology, sing me pulverized
tortuga shields. Excavate estivations, quench these xeric
conditions. Sing me shined boots and accordions in the placita
where a gondola waits to rocket us above cottonwoods.

In arboreal light we glimpse our bone shadows below, fringed
with gold fibers, shimmying and mango-hued, two dirtied
stones, consumed.

WRITE TO THE LIGHTS

that twinkle only in your blinking to keep contacts from
drying under the canopy of el paso sky where quails run
across a dirt path and fly, momentarily, to hide in an
evergreen while you pass blue and red handprints on a
styrofoam paperplate, a child's artwork not so tough for the
child but an artifact of factual for you. how easy it was to dip
nature into paint and print it. how easy it is to stop writing,
crack open another one and demand entertainment. how easy
to read about the past in photographs, in soft skin from our
20's without so much worry set in, but then again worry
manifested itself always in the belly. poke us and feel all
softness, poke us and feel all nothingness. poke the past and
find different versions of our selves. when studying
photographs of children we too easily determine "that is their
core—that expression"—when examining ourselves we
lament what used to be, or herald what is, in comparison.

juárez, a steady stream of walkers over the river. juárez, with
pink crosses for too many murdered women. juárez, with
chinese food i never tasted. juárez, i could list all that you
could do for me as so many others have lit your red
firecrackers before with pockets full of coins and none left for
the picket signs brushed by a child's hands. kennedy, did you
ask your lovers what you could do for them? did you love
marilyn enough to breathe her in mornings after make-up and
perfume—breathe her in between? i want to breathe in the
wet dirt of snake paths and turtle entrances. i want to breathe
in the gulf's salt water, that warmth now part of my
consciousness. breathe in creeley's lines for the delight of
mediocrity gone musical, beautiful. i admit it, i'm a sucker for
well-placed line breaks, rhythm and sound. a slant rhyming
couplet at the end of a non-rhyming effort will get me every
time. i want to ration the irrational in earthquake cans,
hurricanes. x marks the duct tape spot where windows won't
break into a zillion crystals. x marks the spot where the tree
trimmer fell the wrong tree then finished off the wounded one
hiding behind the fence. red marks the spot where the

possum played dead then died. i never saw her in waking life, the big rata of telephone wires and acorns. i called you, x, so many times in writing. sometimes i call you homey when phones tap dance and breathe like patriots. i never woke up to feel awake or dying. i've died to wake but not with intention or celebration.

Donna Perkins

OUR BED

Irritations develop
Teeth
Itch, burrow, bite

Then sex—
Rain
Falling on parched earth

Jere Pfister

BURN UNIT ENTRY - 1985

I sit by her bed and listen as the young mother tells me how she awoke to the fire. How, still not fully awake she put her hand through the wall and brought back fire. She tells how she searched for her son. "He must be at one of the neighbors. You know how boys are," she reassures me, herself. Charred skin, shades of blue, red, and purple show through the cracked blisters that erupt from her face, black on black with underlying color, like a Rothko canvas. I retreat.

A nurse with scars from another fire, comforts me in the room where dead skin washes away in swirling bathtubs. We sit on the edges of the tubs that are back to back and look out the windows at the beauty of falling snow. The cold and snow are the underlying cause behind the house fire that has brought the three of us together.

The nurse excuses himself and returns with a gift. A snowball gathered from the empty life flight pad. I place it on a shelf inside the small refrigerator used to cool the beer that washes down the morphine that numbs the pain of the baths. The woman's son is dead. In the morning, they find his body inside the chimney where he sought shelter from the fire.

Robert Phillips

NOTHING'S AS IT SHOULD BE

The pie is not easy.
The pin is not neat.
The bees are not busy.
The milk is not meek.

The hound, not lazy.
The clams aren't happy.
The loon is not crazy.
The friend-in-need, snappish.

The cat piss is not mean.
The thieves are not thick.
The hound's tooth is not clean.
The winks are not quick.

The fiddle is not fit.
The bells, never clear.
The honey's never sweet.
The three-dollar bill, unqueer.

The molasses isn't slow.
The church mouse, not poor.
The mule, not stubborn in toto.
The ceiling's not another's floor.

The bunny isn't dumb.
The toothache doesn't hurt.
The rail is not thinsome.
The soil's not cheap as dirt.

The grass isn't green.
The horses aren't healthy.
Nothing's right about the rain
God's not in Heaven, all's not OK.

Robert Phillips

TRIANGLE SHIRTWAIST FACTORY FIRE

1911

I, Rose Rosenfeld, am one of the workers
who survived. Before the inferno broke out,
factory doors had been locked by the owners,

>   to keep us at our sewing machines,
>   to keep us from stealing scraps of cloth.
>   I said to myself, What are the bosses doing?
>   I knew they would save themselves.

I left my big-button-attacher machine,
climbed the iron stairs to the tenth floor
where their offices were. From the landing window

>   I saw girls in shirtwaists flying by,
>   Catherine wheels projected like Zeppelins
>   out open windows, then plunging downward,
>   sighing skirts open parasols on fire.

I found the big shots stuffing themselves
into the freight elevator going to the roof.
I squeezed in. While our girls were falling,

>   we ascended like ashes. Firemen
>   yanked us onto the next-door roof.
>   I sank to the tarpaper, sobbed for
>   one-hundred forty-six comrades dying

or dead down below. One was Rebecca,
my only close friend, a forewoman kind to workers.
Like the others, she burned like a prism.

Relatives of twenty-three victims later brought suits.
Each family was awarded seventy-five dollars.
It was like the Titanic the very next year—
No one cared about the souls in steerage.

Those doors were locked, too, a sweatshop at sea.
They died due to ice, not fire. I live in
Southern California now. But I still see

skirts rippling like parachutes,
girls hit the cobblestones, smell smoke,
burnt flesh, girls cracking like cheap buttons,
disappearing like so many dropped stitches.

John Poch

METAPHORS OF LUBBOCK

In the street, pigeons besiege french fries.
They are like women on a smoke break
outside a metal door at the gas company.
Full of hankering, they let their cigarettes ash
and ash, seeming to say, *We are far from love.*

The women look up. The corners
of the buildings are griffin-less.
One woman's brain feels to her
as dry as sheet metal.
She could cry out at any moment.

Yet, the sheet metal, from afar,
in the orange light of a windy late afternoon,
is like an orange detail
of a color field painting
by Frank Stella at MOMA.

Frank Stella, with his shaped canvases
of unremarkable colors and his parallel lines,
is like the father I never had.
The father I never had is my father.

John Poch

THE LLANO RIVER

In a pile of mesquite wreckage in the field
not far above the river, the cotton rat twitches
in its sleep, dreaming of a Sharp-shinned hawk.
At the river bottom, the giant stands
of pecan trees canopy a trampled deer path
which is its own small stream carried away
with her footsteps. The wind moves through
the grass at the bank like three deer, and then
three deer move through the grass like light wind.
They are three does the color of rotten twine,
and they lift their heads when a single mesquite leaf
shakes loose from its tree fluttering as if
it had wanted this long spiraling downward.
Her path leads from the field to the river,
and I have followed with my book in which
none of this appears, not one wooden giant
or a path or a woman I must follow with my book.

John Poch

THE WINDMILL

Above the world's immensest aquifer,
I stand abandoned like an idiot
struck by the wind, an arrested officer.

Sentence me, Dante, to fruitful tedium.
If I were purged of passive voice, I'd move
myself to irrigation's idiom.

Ravens built a barbed-wire nest above
my steel-backed babbitted bearings. A marbling
runs down my neck from their cloacal uncouth.

The tongues of Ogallala's babbling
should be my glossolalia, my liquid mirth
of humming to drown the rusted warbling

of the black brood stabbing the sky for all they're worth—
a hunger for blood and dust. And though I rest,
a mere old battered scaffold here on Earth,

Texas, due east of Farwell, a wind-gust west
of Plainview's woes, like Bartimaeus, blind,
naked, leaning toward the sun, I confess

conversion thirst in history's gears, the kind
that hold the earth to sky and roar to growl.
Imagine the metal teeth of wind and wind

and not precisely knowing the sound of the vowel
content with being blown until, turning
forward, clockwise with a holy howl:

a blade, then space, a blade, then space, churning
and drawing water from the earth, not oil,
till longhorn drift like snow above the burning

miles of almost useless iron soil.
I'm not James Dean's dirty derrick in *Giant*,
but a windmill, grinding arid air, loyal

to the continent. Utterly un-Hawaiian,
amazed at rain and poet-lonely, I am
this stationary, long-necked, high plains lion.

Deseree Marie Probasco

JACKSON POLLOCK IS DEAD

but I am looking at his soul
dashed across a canvas
that fills a white room
in the Museum of Modern Art.

I have forgotten how to breathe
though I am not yet dying
because the room is breathing
with color
and thick arms of paint
reach out to hold me up.

Lines dance to the edge of the canvas
turning back again and again
unsatisfied and longing
a ravening ocean of hue
barely constrained by eight
blue poles.

He is there among the madness
handprints and cigarettes
tossed among the vivid waves
as beacons for the eye.

I am there among the madness
drowning in a work
with no borders
and these are my lifelines.

BIG BULL AND LITTLE DOG

The bull's head rides the dining room wall with lonely grace.
Its eyes have a no-directions-needed look
and for black glass balls they concentrate an awful lot of
    midnight, deep
glints of regret—why that night wafer in the sky never got
    close enough to lick,
or the grass there was no end to eating no matter how much
got swallowed, and how empty the brain with nothing to
    worship.
A head like this—whose long horns reel off greedily
toward inconsolable horizons; with nostrils so capacious
a soul could easily depart from one for a little out-of-bull
    escapade
and in one breath return through the other—a head like this,
the size of a small planet, could easily tire of pulling its body,
an entire universe of mystery, so that who could blame it
for one day lying down on the land and sighing,
with a big self-expelling snort, *Enough.*

Outside three white dogs begin at one end of the neighbor's
    yard
and run the slight length of it back and forth along the fence,
following a little dog on the other side the way particles follow
    a magnet.
Prancing and whirling, the little dog doesn't know its own
    power,
how maybe it had been a spirit on its way to divinity,
having learned the bigger lessons of pursuing hope, fleeing
    despair,
before getting stalled on the ground, thinking, "What fun
to inhabit a little dog and chase around
not for money, or blood, no abracadabra,
just a good romp up and down the cyclone fence, not asking
why it's named for disaster, just dashing

and brushing the grass with the ease of a shadow.
The three dogs sound diminutive until the little dog replies
with a toy-piano rendition of bow-wow, wow-wow,

and although perhaps musically precocious, even the little dog
    knows nothing
of the bull floating in its first language—silence—which is also
    its last
and the last language of all the lost and all the scattered, and
    knows nothing
of the silence of bones and skulls,
the last of me, the last of you.

MOONSHINE

Out here in the backyard, we're watching the moon to see if
    it's closer,
brighter, bigger, anything special, being it's the last fullness
on the last solstice at the end of the millennium,
and though it looks the same, it's bathing everything in the
    kind of light
you notice when you think this is it, the end of something, a
    glow
you want to inhale, hoping it will make you light-hearted.
Moonlight has turned the sky an adolescent blue,
backlighting the winter trees so they overhang
the yard with black lace. It's turning the rubber factory
    Tuscan colors
so that it rises over our streets like a castle.
If the moon were fauna, it would be a goat.
If the moon were a tool, it would be the little mirror the dentist
    uses
to see what's wrong with your teeth. If it were ten thousand
    small things
it would be bubbles in champagne, always rising.
Amazing how much the moon can do with borrowed light,
with emptiness, when today all the talk is about money.
If the moon were silver it would be a gaze ball
in the big garden of space, reflecting the earth in miniature.
If the moon were flora it would be the spent cup
of a meadow beauty after the bloom is gone.
It's a long way from Tuscany to the neighborhood church
and the marquee that claims "The Saints: God's
    Handkerchiefs."
If the moon were a pill, maybe it would be God's aspirin.
It's December, but warm enough to be outside without coats.
    We're trying
and failing to feel the passage of time in the slight breeze,

trying and failing to imagine the next moon filling in the next
   century.
The pecan trees reach long and languorous toward some
   hosanna
in the highest, the roots of the oldest set down in the days of
   the dark enslavement.
Where's the handkerchief, the saint, the God for that?

DAMAGE

You could remember the house you were born in.

You could remember the red voice of the sea.

You could be hours driving down a freeway in someone else's
     car.

You could be crossing a desert in a Western no one's seen but
     you.

You could roll down the windows and let the sunshine kick
     your cheeks.

You could open your mouth real wide.

You could ask a silent question.

You might watch mirages lift off the asphalt like somebody's
     silly theory about time.

You might count the tumbleweeds, adding up the numbers in
     your head.

Your thoughts could float like ashes in the air.

You could memorize the rules or you could break them like
     knitting needles.

You could imagine your mother.

You could drive through a wall of smoke.

After miles of road and rolling plateau, you might reach a
     fading white adobe church.

You might get out of the car to stretch your legs a little.

Maybe you'd walk inside that place of worship, dip your
     finger into an urn of cold water, and make a bullet-shaped
     drop on your own forehead.

Maybe you'd sing a passionate song to the stained glass.

Maybe a woman would glide up behind you like a childhood
     memory of wind.

She might ask you if you lost your lamp.

She might make a prediction about weather.

You could tell her you know her.

You could read the messages zooming out of her eyes.

She might pound on your chest until the feathers flew out.
She might steal your name.

You might rush back to your car, feeling afraid, feeling
    changed.
You might examine your reflection in the rear view mirror and
    wonder why the picture won't stay still.
You might spit in the dust before you start your car.
You might touch your body all over, making sure that it's still
    okay.

Pray. Pray with me.

You could evolve.
You could make the desert your conquest.
You could seed the earth, a thousand paper cranes released
    along the highways we call America.
You could drive through the sun.
You could write down your version of everything you've
    done.
You could lie.
You could love me.
You could turn the page.

Robin Reagler

THE GRIEF SNAPSHOT

One day I saw a sign

BLACK DOG WHITE FACE

stapled to a telephone pole.

I was just walking around, and

the photo stared right at me.

Does this lost dog look familiar?
Yes, I'm thinking he does.

Oh, the loud, echoey spaces!
The empty parking lot!

IN HIDING

I don't remember
ever actually falling asleep
in the old mulberry . . . guess
I could have, but my heart
was usually pumping
pretty desperately
after each narrow escape
(from any number of imagined enemies)
into that towering robin hood world.

Once, I was a chameleon
lying in the saddle
at the juncture
of two mammoth limbs
that reached out over the driveway
and saw a man
who was so lonesome
he carried an empty bud vase, hoping
someone would put a rose in it.

John E. Rice

GOOGLING CHARON

Charon has a web-site, I'll bet
you didn't know that. You can go
to www.styxclyx.com. He's set
up with an Email link, too, y'know—
it's Charon@onewayferry.com. I was wary
at first, all that mythological crap
even bible-thumpers don't believe—and it's scary
contacting a demon. What if it was a trap
or some kind of parallel universe down there?
But I tried it anyway. I mean I do have my own
demons to confront and they're bad enough: bare-
assed, hairy, fanged, foaming-at-the-mouth, home-grown
devils right out of my tiny hyperactive mind—
but Charon, he's the real thing, not Memorex,
and I like boats, too, he just runs another kind.
I kept it simple, no question too complex,
after all, you don't want to get Old Charon pissed!
I just asked for a look at his passenger list.

Sally Ridgway

HARDLY WORTH MENTIONING

for Laura Guidry

that squirrel dead in our street
the one that sharpened its teeth on the white antlers on the
    balcony

the resonance of its gnawing
bone on bone on the balcony floor,
friends cocked their heads in wonder
at the sound in our still house

I'd tell them it was our squirrel brushing her teeth
do you want to see?
no, they'd say, but I did—
antlers I'd placed there, the squirrel leaping rooftops to find them
me, watching from my morning window

then the squirrel headed for the neighbor's maple
and a car racing, no doubt, oblivious . . .

        *   *   *

the sky is bone white behind the maple
my silent morning ritual, the white structure of the antlers

I want something the same each morning
unconscious, unimportant—trivial sound, insignificant
time
while big things drop off that were unnatural anyway

I'd lifted the antlers from a forest floor, admiring their lines,
hauled them home, a thousand miles,
art for three balconies, two marriage's worth, a quarter
    century

until that daily sound of determined life,
my part—provision, witness,
now the sunrise behind the maple is pink as if suffused
with the tiniest drop of blood

Daniel Rifenburgh

Codicil To Be Appended To The City Charter

I remember liberating with difficulty her white
Breasts from the brassiere. We were coming of age

In the leafy woods of young mammals.
Later, we moved to the city

And were given jobs and instruction. Industry hummed.
You could buy a color tv, drapes. There was nothing

That could not be insured against loss.
Some people spent whole days in offices

Writing up the policies, charmed by the reasonableness
The ages had granted human affairs.

These were among those most taken aback
When that noble lady, the mother of the king,

Held by its mane what she thought was
The severed head of a lion, but when she looked closer

It was the head of her son. He had given offense
To a vine-wreathed god, and the god had put

A special madness on her. With bloody hands
She quit the plaza and sped into exile,

Wailing beyond the walls of the city
But where had been woods was now wasteland

And in that desert she fed only on heartbreak
And soft, plaintive cries of the panthers.

Daniel Rifenburgh

ON EPSTEIN'S STATUE "JACOB AND THE ANGEL" AT THE TATE GALLERY

Clearly, by dawn, the struggle is over,
The contest ends, and the angel has won.

What of the snaking caravan
Of cattle, folk, and possessions Jacob
Sent before him across the muddy river?

How will he reach it, thus defeated,
With his thigh bone out of its hip socket
(The angel's last, gymnastic maneuver),

So that he now cannot even arise
To his former stature, but must be propped
By the brace of arms wrapping his torso?

(But his thoughts are not on his possessions;
Rather, he has demanded a blessing.)

He, prior to this moment seen
Carved in alabaster, the very
Embodiment of the word, *insistent,*

Clasping the stranger, this man or angel,
The one who calls himself. "Why do you ask
My name?" and not letting go of him till

At last, just now, the winged being bent
Over Jacob and gave up his blessing,
Saying, "Now you shall be called by all
Peoples, *Who Struggles With God.*"

Here, in the moment just after that moment
The collapse, the letting go,

But, with a new name, as if a new man
And the tall angel, that greater power,
Does not let go the newly blessed man,

But supports him while the great name invades
His thigh bone to the marrow, by the joint
Of the hip, as if thus to prepare him

For the centuries to come,
As if all the freight, all the barges, of all
Of the rivers of the world will end here in this

Frail figure, an *agon* of a man,
This struggling thing, this injured, insistent name
Clasping this god
And the god clasping him.

For Annie Freud

Erika Rodriguez Hernandez

MRS.

When her husband died
she stopped cooking and sweeping.
She ate fruits and vegetable
and cold water
raw.

The floor became lightly covered
in dust, then dirt
tracking her steps
up and down the stairs
and her dance
around the deep mahogany
office desk.

Her insanity was gradual
as a storm that begins
with a cloud of black birds
rising from a tree.

She stopped wearing shoes.
Then peeled stockings off her legs
like washing the wax off an apple.
Her shirt became undone and
Her skirt fainted into a puddled
dark halo for her feet.

She unhooked the hammock
around her breasts.
The last pale sliver of her underclothes
sank like a morning moon
beneath the horizon.

She took a fine box of long white gloves
and reached her hand into their fingertips
looking for treasure
in their hidden unworn silk.

In gloves and nothing
she fixed the typewriter—oily black—
and typed.

That's how they found her
wearing a black ink smudge
just under her pursed pink lips'
locked smile.

Erika Rodriguez Hernandez

POET KISSING PICASSO

my lips went to his lips
but kissed the shell of his ear.

his fingers are long blades of grass
sculpting winds in an open meadow.
I am sleeping in his hands
like a cup of tea left behind at a picnic.

when he is finished painting,
it is not me.
my neck is an empty glass vase—
he draws it as a single shard of glass.
my wrists are melting ice—
he makes them crying hinges.
my forearms are the underbellies of flying fish—
he catches them in hungry sleeves.

I am a painting.
Beautiful, he says, taking
me in his arms
which are only arms.
"Por eso to amo."

Iris Rozencwajg

WHERE

was your father liberated? asked the old man
at the reunion. Three generations, maybe
four, sat around looking
out over a swimming pool. My father,
I said slowly, was not
detained. He left earlier. *Where
did he live then?* asked the man.

He lived in the West Indies, I answered,
working for Standard Oil. *And he
stayed there? made a living?* He made
a living, I said, near the devil's
pawn shop, making deposits of treasured
anguish to have something for us
to live on, and then, life
being what it was, redeeming
it when things changed. Soon
enough, feeling destitute, he'd return,
receiving yet again half
what it was worth until
the next time he'd take it back.

My father, Sir, died as it were
in custody. *Did he play
soccer?* asked the man. A fanatic,
I said, and known for it.

I too, said the man. *Tell him my name.
He'll know me.*

BURYING

I found him stumbling about when the mother
died, an otherwise healthy calf, and fed him
by bottle until another cow came due, then
moved him in with her for suckling.
Third night she broke his neck.
It was a right and natural thing to do:
She reasoned, if cows can reason,
that her milk was for hers alone.
I found him barely breathing, head thrown
back, unable to rise for the bottle,
his eyes already hazing over. I could see
myself fading in them, backing into fog.
I brought the pipe down hard, twice, the
second time in malice: not for him or her,
but for the simple nature of things.
Blood came from his nose, his body
quivered. I dragged him from the barn.
The hole in the winter garden was easy, quick,
and the calf fit properly; but when the
first shovel of dirt struck his side,
he kicked, with vigor. I watched the flailing
foot strike against air. Nothing else moved.
There were no considerations: I did what
needed to be done. A few more scoops clamped
the leg and the earth stilled. I mounded
the grave and turned away, looking back once
to see that nothing heaved. I felt neither
fear nor sorrow, love nor hate. I felt
the slick handle of the shovel, slid
my thumb over its bright steel blade,
breathed deep the sharp and necessary air.

Paul Ruffin

LLANO ESTACADO: THE NAMING

When Coronado and his three hundred
soldiers and six hundred Pueblo slaves
pursued El Turco across this grand plateau,
he could not have known what he had entered
until mile after trackless mile they followed
their phantom prey and found on all sides
the same stretch of grass and sky,
only at night orienting themselves, gazing
at the same stars men steer their ships by,
constellations they had known before
their ascent into a shadeless hell.

In this land of alkaline waters, broken
by sudden ravines that yawned hotly open
as if the earth would swallow them,
the plated soldiers rode, sweltering
in the merciless sun, the shimmering air.
Some fell, clattering, never to rise again,
some threw their armor aside and faced the sun.

Behind them, where nearly a thousand had passed,
the grass closed like water and all about them
was nothing but the sameness of the grassy sea.
So in time they came to cut from stunted trees
that lined dry washes poles to mark their way.
Mile after mile they drove the sticks
as they moved, stakes that leaned in the wind,
trailing out behind them, monuments to their folly,
telling them nothing of where they were going
and little of where they had been.

Benjamin Alire Sáenz

KNOWLEDGE: THE HAND OF ANOTHER

> *He knows that in spite of all the stout talk of his fellows*
> *he must live and die in uncertainty, a thing blown*
> *by the winds, a thing destined like corn to wilt in the*
> *sun.*

—*Sherwood Anderson*

In the winter light, books open—
Pages, words becoming shadows, the room
Growing darker, sober, sadder, a dark and tragic
Stage. Caesar, Iago, Brutus, Lear perform
Soliloquies, still lifes of murderous
Intents, distilled for years in vats of seductive
Fermenting iambics—words, sentences, nouns,
Pronouns, verbs—and how is it that we
Learn to put letters, words together
Organize them as if with that alone
We could rearrange the sad and tired
Universe? As if with words alone we could
Undo the damage we have inflicted
With our guns that are more beloved
Than the sincere and saccharine tears
We shed at the first note of the *Star*
Spangled Banner before the pitcher throws
Out his first slider. If we can alphabetize
A library, why not the gardens and rooms
We inhabit? Why not the stars? Why not
The scattered peoples of the earth?
I would one day like to alphabetize
The emotional lives of my brothers and sisters—
And for one blessèd moment believe
That order is more than a myth invented
By an eighth century priest with too much

Time on his hands. A cloud is passing. I am
Watching the cloud as I stare out
The window. A passing cloud is a fiction,
A lazy and cheap description of what is actually
Happening. Scientists are clearer, more
Disciplined about these matters. The dog
Is barking. I speak to her as if she is
Human, not knowing or caring what
Words mean to her. What can words mean
To a dog? There is the possibility
Her intelligence may be less questionable
Than the complex and confusing formulas
Of scientists and tragic Shakespearean characters.
The dog, at least, does not put her faith
In linguistic or mathematical equations. Her
Vocabulary is small and pragmatic: *bone,
walk, sit.* What is language? What is
Knowledge? I know people who claim to know
How to measure intelligence—a misguided
Way to rank human beings as if they were
Ivy League Universities. I don't know anyone
Who has ever claimed to know how to measure
A human heart. I know people who understand
Politics and God and the deeper subliminal messages
Of movies and the semiotics of the covers
Of all the books on the *New York Times* Bestseller
Lists. Perhaps you *can* tell a book by its cover.
Mrs. Skuba, my fifth grade teacher, would die
If she read what I just wrote. She would sit me
Down in the back of the classroom, force me to
Meditate on what I've become. I'm happy
I became anything. My life could have been
Much worse. And anyway, I'm certain that
Mrs. Skuba is dead, so what does it matter? Other
Things killed her. Certainly, not words. Not mine.

*   *   *

I know people who can tell
The future or the pain of your past
Just by looking at all the lines
in the palms of your hand.
The human hand is a book
Where suffering
Is written in wordless lines.

Tell me again
About the necessity of language.

*   *   *

I am thinking of George Willard, how he left
Winesburg, Ohio. I am wondering how many
Scars he took with him and wonder if Salinger
Wasn't right, after all, when one of the heroes
In one of his books said that he had scars
On his hands from touching the people
He loved. I am thinking Of Wing Biddlebaum,
How the rumors of a town kept him
From touching anyone ever again, spending
All his time trying to hide those things
At the end of his arms he once used
For touching. I am thinking of how Wing
Might have been guilty of all the things
The people of the town thought in their small
And ungenerous minds, how he might have been
A saint, a greater mystic than St. John of the Cross.

*   *   *

My wife breathes softly next to me. I wake, get up,
Let the dog out, drink a glass of water, go back
To bed. I look at my hand and think it a strange
Thing, each finger like a separate word that refuses
To be a part of the same sentence. The stars
Are out, sleepwalking in the darkness of the night.
I make my way back to bed — and for a brief
Second, I touch the hand of my sleeping
Wife. The stars have ceased from their nightly
Wanderings. The moon is waning. The night
Is quiet. I fall asleep. When I wake, her hand is still
There. Like corn, I will wilt in the sun. I do not need
To live forever.

      Her hand. There are moments
When everything is perfect and lyrical.
I know all I need to know.

M. *Duncan Scheps*

LAS VEGAS

I will not love Las Vegas
Until my mother dies
And dies again.
The glitz and razz-matazz
Ka-ching and ring and
Bright casino beats:
Tk-tk-tk-tk. Tk-tk-tk.
So many naked girls
With no qualms
Plastic, phony, made-up, man-made,
Over-the-top
Excess.
Sequined nipples
Are too much for
My Quaker-bred mother
Of practical, taciturn bent—
From women who dry soap
On rafters to make it last
For whom perfume is pine needles
And honeysuckle,
And noise is
A single bee
Roaming over flowers, or
Waves rolling their foamy arms
Along the shore.
Too much for my mother
Such bad behavior
The clatter and roar,
Gilded, silvered, encrusted, bubbling
Swinging to big crescendos
Over and over and over,
Too many, too much
For her, and for me.
She lives inside me (of course)
My mother.
But when she is gone,
We shall see
We shall see.

Kate Schmitt

AFTERWORLD

in memory of my grandparents

My mother finds him sitting on a lawn chair
in the driveway, tapping his foot as blood runs
down his face and into his lap.

A great cloud dome snaps out lightning.
When we know the jig is up
we sit on the porch step

and the pieces fall away.

        *   *   *

I can hear the lightbulbs,
high pitched and terrible.
Tell me about fear,

what she would never say, death leaning
against the window jamb and deciding to watch awhile.
The small *oh* of breath.

What is left: the same rooms
without anyone to see them.
The concrete still warm from day.

        *   *   *

Tiny needle-nosed ghost bird,
the sun is losing light.

You move farther away.
When you turn homeward

everything will have moved.

*   *   *

Days break.
A corner rooftop lit now.
Time = distance.
Reaching back
for the old formulas—*pi* times radius squared
—calculating what halfway through this planet might be.

I can't wait for night
to fall again.
All those hours you disappear.

*   *   *

The moon again, slivered and scary.
Night after night the palm tree fingering
the air with paper claws.

The ghosts come back, walking
memories like old dogs.
I could get a blanket but I don't.
Children chant in the night room:

as I was going up the stair
I met a man who wasn't there;
He wasn't there again today—
and the blinds jail the room with shadows.

You read this and one day you will be breathless.

*   *   *

The metallic taste of raspberries
And the way the word is spelled—*rasp*.

Here, a hole:
summer comes and erases them.
Tadpoles in my heart.

* * *

When the white slips of bloom fall
off your orchids and only green sticks are left
you say, *Wait.* They will come back.
How far ahead
you have to be able to look
to want to keep orchids.

* * *

The last thing is to praise:
thunder shaking the windows and the snail's trail shining
on the patio, never mind that it's come from the basil,
the mint, the sage, the dry part where the grass is dying.

Praise night's dark comma.
Praise runaway sleep who lies homeless
somewhere near the trains, counts
the night sky like a glowing abacus.

Feel the blood tunneling to the knot of heart
at the center. Remember what flowers do
to the secret inside you, how you feel when you see
the birds all fall suddenly

then step onto a wire and hold.

Varsha Shah

RUMINATION I

> *"Be Empty of worrying.*
> *Think of who created thought!*
> *Why do you stay in prison*
> *When the door is so wide open?"*
> —*Rumi translated by Coleman Barks*

As the day surrenders the night,
as the month folds into a year,
the year an era, era to something else—
I begin to see
the door flings open to break its falling
and suddenly
I drop out of my body's sky—a moth exits
the flower's brown edges
earthward—another life.

The muslin moon of evening, a phasing face
watches me—
I become translucent.
Together we circle the track;
My feet take her energy, as
A wren makes the last call to his mate
gathering their youngsters back into nest.
The hibiscus folds up her red umbrella on a distant patio,
once my home;
A quiet glance I feel
pouring from the rooms, street, drip by drip
as the thought flees her prison,
turning into light of my palm.

Varsha Shah

RUMINATION II

> *"I AM all orders of being,*
> *The circling galaxy, the evolutionary intelligence,*
> *The lifting and the falling away..."*
> —*Rumi translated by Coleman Barks*

Says Time:

Yesterday I was at the Eros cinema
sipping cold coffee, drunk with Gulzar's gazals
pretending you were saqi
sealing my mouth
with sharabi eyes.

It was a crack in the mirror—
Or, was it a dream?
Lift your surahi and toast to who I am,
Come, step into my beat, and dance—now
Let my arms be your galaxy.

Some call me death,
Some see me beside the riverbank.
I am the front and the back,
The body inside **nobody**.

Don't wait till you'll know me, *then*—
surrogate for today.
Tomorrow is the empty shell, your pretense for living.

LOVE ME

as if we'd defined the word freedom
found its translation in five senses,
    two bodies, the peculiar
language of barbed wire

as if we'd rendered it a translucent crow
perched on a burning sun
    winging red across horizons
releasing inherent suggestions of flight

not refugees, not wounded children
not guerrilleros in wars of clashing
    priorities
not man and woman or world

we will be eyes and hands and touch
heavy with the creation of leaf-ing seeds
    dizzying light become sustenance
revolving in the fierce space before bones

THE WIND SUFFERS LOVE

       i know how to love shadows
drifting fog crow's wings skeletal
branches against a purple darkness
faraway lamplight and the echoes of
voices my love is a weary thing sighing
and bleeding collapsing and bubbling
my love is too strained for flesh flesh is
impossible flesh keeps escaping me my
hands must be made of wind

       escape me leave me my mouth filling
with black whirlwinds i choke on dust and
unrequited my untouched skin cooling scaling
over flesh gone rock gone vicious with
forsaking black spiders of renunciation live in
my belly spinning webs of disconsolation

       i loved you even leaving my
lips shaping your name with longing
even as the wind seeded curses inside
me bitter wind clinging to memories of
ruptured bliss harsh wind that makes
of us leaves scraping over asphalt rabid
wind maddened and frothing
scorching the earth and uprooting
tenderness

       sweep through me wind losing none of
your grey ferocity hunt out this aching
darkness claw pierce make it whimper cast it
out sweep through me hurling out shadow and
ash loss and wanting leave me loveless wind
leave me luminous light pouring in through my
abandoned eyes my abandoned arms

Eva Skrande

THE PLOWMAN

I wish I was a plowman,
   so an ox, snout big and wide like God, could lead me
to my mother's eyebrows in the red clay,
   as only an ox who knows earth as its wife could.

After the dry, the wintery wet, sowing
   we'd find my mother among the rows of spring.
Amidst this or that seed of chance, we'd look for crows
   borrowing her shoulders, burnt and frayed

because for their own paintings of roses,
   trees love burnt fingers, because fire becomes them
becomes the lips of their families.
   Plowing, the ox pulls the stockings off its lover's roots

and finds life, wildness, that ecstasy of thoughts and spring
   crops
   by its black legs where the dirt falls
in love, o ox, o bridge,
   this hunger for mother, unearths, uncontrols.

Larue Smith

A SLIVER OF LIFE

Terrified, I hold my breath and wait for the silent beat of moth
    wings,
the quiet smoke of the opium den, the dashed delirium of
    dreams gone astray.
All this because a sliver of life has shimmered deep into the
    night
to sit beside me like the withered face of a gauze wrapped
    crone.

This thickness, this stasis of darkness, this twelfth hour
    smothered
in swastika black, thunders, blindfolds . . . rolls me like a
    Russian
tumbleweed. I am stonewalled against a night of Bergman
    beginnings,
and all you can say is . . .
                 shush . . .

                 come lie down
                 the sheets are cool

                 the honeysuckle sweet
                 against the window sill.

Loueva Smith

SWARM

Can you see my heart from here?
How it hangs a swarm of bees
from the thin forgers of the fig tree
at your upstairs window,
and bends and trembles the leaves.
Can you hear the thrumming urgency
of what I ask of you?
With my hind legs I am knitting honey.
My heart is a naked engine of bees.
Answer me with throats of flowers.

Allison Smythe

SOMETHING IN MY EYE

The world is writ in braille but our hands
are tied behind our backs with finest cashmere.
And yet somehow we know:

rivers wait for no one, mountains do not mourn,
there are no circles under the eyes of the ancient
hills nor will the silent canyon remember

when you walked it. Between spank and breath
the orchid of mortality is delivered, an unsigned
card pinned to the stem, the memory

of a kiss. The world is repeatedly stained
with ink spilled at twilight. When even dumb
cities bloom without regret like gladiolas

before they wither, what does it mean to wear
flesh, to learn the name of the dark
birds assembled on the wire like beads

on a rosary, time always running out
like a lover sprinting for the bus, the first

drops of 10,000 year old rain just beginning
to darken the lapel of his fine woolen coat.

Allison Smythe

WHEN I SNAP MY FINGERS YOU'LL WAKE UP

and you won't remember a thing. *As if.*
As if the Atlantis sunk inside you is not

a tampering ghost, moving margins,
blurring boundaries, hiding words

under your tongue like keys
to the front door. Leaving

lights on, a ring
in the tub, the phone off the hook.

Scribbling the unwalked world in
day by day in pencil.

In this life only birds rise
high enough to detach

their shadows, projecting simple
negatives of themselves

onto a ceiling paved
in light. But we, heavy-footed,

are stalked by shadows
that mock each gesture,

anticipate each move, pin us
to concrete, dirt, mown grass.

Our hands, stamped with invisible
expiration dates, always

sticky from cupping all this
unsolved beauty and the devastation

of alternate endings.
Once

Aristotle dreamt the heavens
spun around the earth

the way the glutted dream
of lack. He could not yet calculate

the length of a summer on Pluto
or how many millimeters,

at any given moment,
one might hover from disaster.

But he knew the ruin
of plenty, preaching a fearful

symmetry attained only by sleep-
walkers who, upon awakening,

forget each unmapped journey.
Now, as then, birds spin

around the earth, caught
in its gravity. Their small shadows

overlap ours, which absorb,
for that passing moment,

their immaculate renditions of flight.

Michael Sofranko

HAPPY TO HAVE IT

Until I grew weary of watching
the surfacing carp
stop just this side of the Milltown bridge
to feed on whatever floats,
I thought I might die among the immigrant
workers, or worse yet, live on forever,
nursed like their stagnant steins of beer.
The willows failed along the red,
eroding banks, and I found the pain
unbearable as I watched, so at not even
seventeen, I dropped the lead bible
in the land of their failed labor and walked out.
We might have gone as far as Lot,
my loss and I. We might have tethered at
the exotic docks, but instead drifted
through waves of prairie fire and plain talk.
We might have settled there, married the homilies
and the honest life, but banked instead
nothing of what we earned or stole,
and small gossip spread the stale news
each time we eloped. My loss and I,
spread thin as the gospel, finally preached
to the damned infuriated
heat one summer, circa 1985.
It listened and replied, *You have had your say.*
Now I will swallow you. And as the bright noon
startled the debris at the edge
of Houston, the swamp girl who can't stop
spreading her skirts, I wavered
like the oversized flag, half hanging
its head in the insufferable calm. And each
night since I've been happy to have it,
all of it: the toothless miners, my landlord Ohio,

the brittle, biting eucalyptus branches,
and the small touch of a hand
reaching across the white sheet.
For even the empty hours, I'm grateful.
Happy to have it, all of it.
Happy to have it; happy to let it go.

JUST ASK ME

Some drought-stricken August
In front of the old theater
The letters askew on the sagging marquee

Ask how the little pieces
That once composed my self
Broke off and fell to the shoulder

The last time I tried to take the right road
And migrate again from my own
Stale breath. Ask where the key

To the map of my face resides,
How shame drew ploughs
And planted its dirty rows, how lies

Fell into furrows and blossomed
With thorn-bearing berries.
Ask me if the wind ever fooled me

Into thinking I could rise like God
Lifting me off the pavement
Like a paper angel as the ice

Blew in frenzied acres of feeling
At my feet. When we crouch there
Along the quiet debris, just ask me

What I hope to find when I stare
At the dance hall, dead in the sun,
Or squint at the heat devils

Spinning their fumes
From the empty street.
They are reminders: that I am one

Of the strays; I say what they say,
The old dogs that bay at the sky
In their longing and moonlight.

DONALD JUDD'S HANGAR

Marfa, Texas

Owls in scrawled cedars overlook
the courtyard. Artists inside, out
of their heads.

They have quit the city
or traveled between there and here
where nowhere is

where land is juke joint
or cathedral, and their response is illusion
lost in the notes.

No sensible structure, this hangar
(crimped steel on hardened ground, sun-annealed)
open for revels

most summer evenings. Voices
from the crowd, lyric over the superheated plains,
insinuate themselves into

dreams of boxes (one hundred,
aluminum) painting the desert as it alters slightly
every quarter hour.

Sandi Stromberg

DISPLACED PERSON

He wore Russian winters in his eyes,
his mind filled with the smell of borscht
and, pinned to his sleeve, a longing
for the crowded boulevards and language
of his youth. He talked about his days
as a DP, the streets of New York,
his attempts to imitate an American
man's loose-hipped walk. Professor
in an after-thought Russian department
in a Midwestern town, he lost us
with Slavic sibilants, a maze of words
that dead-ended in our blank stares
and made him shout. Sad progeny
of overstuffed lives, we were disappointments,
unattuned to the subtleties of his mother
tongue or how he survived Siberian
camps and a cancer ward. We couldn't connect
with his gulag past though we sensed
his misfitness in the way he clutched —
between index finger and yellowed thumb —
unfiltered cigarettes. In a land of waste,
he savored each puff down to the ember,
focused on a distance we could never traverse.

CURANDERA, HEALER

Your low, *mesquite*-wind voice
whistles softly through half a lung
and cracks like dried leaves in ancient bottles.
Patient teas, potent herbs
stand ready in dusty jars along your kitchen shelves
and in the crowded cabinets of your well-aged mind
where *remedios* older than *árboles*
overlap histories with miracles
and love with labor.
Memory leaves not one space to waste or out of grace.
Lemon rinds, *comino* seeds, reborn in dessicated age,
grow to their purpose, stronger now.
Ojos de venado speak the haunting tenderness
of deer, the power of justice.

Your half-blind eyes whisper prayers through rippled light,
sifting sunshine through the sounds of centuries.
Shuffling slippers pause . . .
Barking dogs bow quiet for this Mass . . .

Hot with blessing
your hands exceed
the boundaries of their bones
and reach
to make
the cure.

Carmen Tafolla

FEEDING YOU

I have slipped *chile* under your skin,
    secretly wrapped in each *enchilada*,
    hot and soothing,
    carefully cut into bitefuls for you as a toddler,
    increasing in power and intensity as you grew
    until it could burn
    forever

    silently spiced into the rice
    soaked into the bean *caldo*
    smoothed into the avocado

    I have slipped *chile* under your skin,
    drop by fiery drop
    until it ignited
    the sunaltar fire
    in your blood

I have squeezed *cilantro* into the breast milk,
    made sure you were nurtured with the taste
    of green life and corn stalks
    with the wildness of thick leaves
    of untamed *monte*
    of unscheduled growth

I have ground the earth of these *Américas* in my *molcajete*
    until it became a fine and piquant spice,
    sprinkled it surely into each spoonful of food
    that would have to expand to fit your soul

Dear Son
Dear Corn *Chile Cilantro* Son

This
is your *herencia*
This
is what is yours
This
is what your mother fed you
to keep you
alive

Jessica Tarrand

LOST IN SPACE

"You're father is a space cadet" my mom used to say
As she took the burning noodles off the stove
Closed the gaping doors
Wrote the late checks.

And for the longest time I thought
He washed the smell of galaxies off his hands
After work lay his head on the table
Plates like black holes
And stared at the satellites to see
Friends working the late shift.

Larry D. Thomas

HOUSEFLY

On an anvil
of light,
with the iron

of iridescence,
her weightless wings
were forged.

Death
beguiles her so
she lays

in what it claims
her cherished eggs.
She's the woman

of the house
of ubiquity.
For her eyes

alone, Picasso
would have sold
his taurine soul.

Larry D. Thomas

WINTER TREES

The sky is overcast, glaring,
as if God were holding the earth
uncomfortably close
to a giant fluorescent light.

In stillness they're suspended there,
bereft of a single leaf,
all bark and verticality,
their thick sap rumbling in their roots

like the crude of capped wells.
They loom like shirtless prisoners,
hoisted in shackles to their toe tips,
braced for the blue, inexorable

scourges of wind and ice,
assuaged but momentarily
with the unguentary
roosting of the vultures.

Stephanie Thome

VAQUERO, I KNOW THE NAME OF THE GAME

You can try to tame bull into lamb,
tangle me in your noose—
you, with your kerchief mask,
but I know the name of the game.

In fact, I already have
my hands and skirt up in surrender—
all round-up for the taking.

It's a shame leather hands like yours
don't know what to do with delicate things.

Gail Tirone

IF MARY SAID NO ...

What if Mary said no
said thanks but no thanks
childbirth really isn't on my agenda
it's not compatible with my career goals
and besides
this is no great deal
nine months of bearing
the sacred weight
twenty-four hours of excruciating labor
years of persecution
followed by a life of mourning
and beatitude expressing itself
in millions of cheap blue-robed
plaster of paris statues
and a few transcendent faces
by Raphael.

MODEL "A" FORD

Grandfather's Sunday car
    Carried Grandma
To Mount Carmel's
    Red brick temple.

His Monday car
    Doubled as a truck
Kept in the barn-shop
    Behind the chicken coop.

On the road to work
    It was loaded with tools
Sawdust and lumber,
    Sometimes Billy.

On a hot night
    The barn-shop burned.
The tools, sawdust and
    Model A Ford died that year.

On a cold night
    The old man fell.
In the morning Bill
    Lifted him to the bed

And sent him home
    To the burnt out Ford,
Bleached out chicken coop
    And the yard
At Mount Carmel's
    Red brick temple.

Evangelina Vigil-Piñón

CIELO Y LUMBRE

to the memory of Ricardo Sánchez, Chicano Poet of El Chuco, c/s

this was your world
cloudless skies
brazen silence
under the hellish sun of El Paso
its monument the cold stone Cristo Rey
with its veil of snow, pines and torturous terrain
jagged rock and matorrales
its apex the white cross
planted like a tree

the solar flares intensify
fierce white rays blind me
thick, curled pointed thorns tear at my knees
the needles of nopales lance my palms and fingers
send sharp pain
a rattle snake stuns me
fear is poison in my blood
I freeze

your world tortures me
I am crawling on all fours a beast
my hands are blood and sand
fileros de piedra slash my palms
deepening the lines of destiny
solar flares erupt
flames burn higher
white rays fiercer

my lips are sea salt
dry and cracked like the land
I am advancing

it is cold
I am ascending
I am alone
the wind howls
I cannot breath
the mountain spins
now I know for sure there's no mistake
I am certain
the white cross has never been about some god

how many times, Ricardo?
how many times did you gaze up at its peak?
a solitary boy beholding the majesty cloudless spacious skies
a man-child harboring la ilusión
a chuco from el Barrio del Diablo breeding desesperación
the everyman raging for liberación
la cruz de los cuatros vientos
etched in your consciousness
tus ojos de águila
penetrating all
and nothing:

solazo cielo lumbre soledad azul sin nubes

Randall Watson

PERISHABLES

They shall be thanked for their softness,
Just as these fingers shall be
                    when they are steep with light,
Just as the feet shall be
                    for their tripping and sliding.

And the moon, too, shall be thanked, for its changes.

And the engines of airplanes that roar toward sleep
    on the edges of that changing light,
And sleep for the rest it gives
When we are broken by the wakefulness of thought,
                    the weight of addition.

Just as the horror of my mother's face shall be thanked
    when she takes her teeth out.

And the heat shall be thanked, for rising.

And I shall thank the cold for coming down,
And the zero shall be thanked
                    for subtracting nothing.

And someone will be there to assist me in this.

And he shall help me thank the hollow of a band shell
    for its wet face.
And he shall help me thank the voice of a man
    who clears his throat in the morning,
And the insect the amateur entomologist pries open,
And the instruments of the entomologist's fingers.

And he will be standing there and he will be my grandfather.

And there will dirt upon his overalls and his gray cap,

And he will tell me what comes, and what comes after,
And he will thank the hands of the pitcher plants
    for their syrupy fingers,
And the steeple of the bittern's face when it glances upwards,
    and we shall do this together.

And then one day he will not be standing.

And the morning will be there in his place
And it will make the world loud with its twitterings
And I will not be fond of its loudness,
I will want the night to close, like a dog's coat,
                        sleek and Labrador,
And I shall want to come undone, like the laces of a shoe,
    before the night is over.

But I shall not come undone, though I should like to.

And I shall seat him on a stump among the elms by the creek,
And I will make it hard to see him because the wind has risen
    and the air is dusty.

So I shall imagine him there, chewing on something.

And his hands shall be busy fixing a footstool
And when he is done he will put his feet up
And there will be mud and stickers on his boots
And he shall point to the clouds that circle above us
And he shall tell me about the clash of ions in the air.

And I shall be so happy I shall thank the dirt on my fingers.

I shall thank the turnip for drawing color from the earth,
And I shall take this color into my mouth and match it
    with my tongue,
And it will be like kissing my grandfather,
    like putting my hand in his.

And we shall take a little plastic boat across the creek,

And we shall share a 7-UP because we are thirsty
　　and there will be shade on the water
And all sorts of bugs shall be flying this way and that.

And a heron also shall be walking in the mud at the creek's edge.

And we shall thank the heron's stillness when we are near
　　because it is the stillness of the mind,
And we shall thank its soft retreat when we approach
　　because it is the mind's movement.

And I shall take the halo from its right eye
　　and slip it on my finger,
And it will be like marrying my grandfather,
　　like going down the aisle together.

And I shall take the halo from its left eye and save it for later.

And the right eye shall be used to rebuild
　　the face of my grandfather.

And I shall return the oil to his skin, the part to his hair,
And he will be young again and we will be standing there.

And then I will give him back the halo I have saved for later.

And we will use it to look at the book we have brought to look at.

And the book will be filled with the reproductions
　　of great paintings.

And there will be blood in the paintings, and a yellow light.

And an essay will tell us which of the colors have faded
And which have been cleansed and returned to brightness.

CANTO XX—{LAZARUS SCROLLS}

Lazarus {must have} thought: again we are robbed
of the grave, of sleep.

   His rough hands catching at the muslin
bandages, unwrapping his eyes.

Even his wife's sweeping, the bristles scraping
the dirt floor—even his habit of biting his nails
return immediately, unchanged.

The body keeps decaying in the small ways.

———————

Dawn. His body goes into the uniform like a coffin.

*To be a mailman is to inhabit this emptiness for hours, to disturb
five hundred abandoned lawns, one after another*

Dusk. The lighting of one fluorescent lamp infects
the whole city.

———————

            Lazarus wanders the long white alleys
of the grocery store. You can tell the organic vegetables
by the dirt that clings. Ranunculae in the market near the stem
and leaf fruits, wedges of cheese haphazard on the shelf
looking like vertebrae or stones—
                              fresh scones imperfectly
shaped, scallops pale and raw, or pearled red steak marbled
with fat.
   He takes home enough white bread, a jug of wine,
potatoes for dinner.

The check-out girl does not look up at his wet face.

Later in the movie theater, chair covered in
hole-y red velvet, he watches:

Voce-profundo:
   Cosi Brigitte Bardot vedi
her skin spread against the sea, a boat of body
water cut in half by the shadow, cliff faceted
by sunlight.
recumbent on the water as if a flat plane
cutting water into angles with her body

   "two hours each morning in large curlers . . . hair coiled
against the fabric . . . Her hair as of translucent amber,
coiffed, done up, and sprayed."

A pleasure to watch the turning back. A pleasure to watch
her languid and bloody in the car at the end.
A pleasure reclining.

   He has seen her in press shoots
for the opening night; {she is} resurrected in white.

JACQUES-LOUIS DAVID COUNSELS HIS PUPILS TO DRAW FROM
   NATURE AS IT IS SHOWN IN THE PANORAMAS:

In L.'s bag:

circulars, newsletters, past-due bills, coupons, notification of
possible wins, of births, of death, of a defunct will, mail
returned from an empty house, mail returned from the
deceased, returned to the deceased, postcards mailed from an
improvised vacation, something soiled by coffee or salt water,
envelopes licked with dry tongues, the last of a woman's
handwriting, the mail-order dildo, the catalogue for
morticians, the latest fashions shot in color on a beach.

———————

He pushes at the sidewalk with his feet, as if rowing.
On cue, the rain begins, on cue the dog barks.

    Since the resurrection his neighbors step back
when he opens the box or the gate, step back when he
    approaches
the community diving board.

    At first, hands from everywhere
    clutching the polyester suit sleeves and shoelaces—stolen
      immediately

He cannot even show a badly shot video
to the curious ones.

By the end of the summer, the neighborhood fills with rumors
    of his halitosis, his mothball suits, the strange keening in
    the living room rising from his television set.

———————

He quits going to the local church

though the whispers suddenly rise into
the sound of wings flapping

———————

{or pigeons on the roof}

———————

L.'s diary:

*—just another strange journey—abandoned bus station in another
town, car broken down on someone else's road—terrible unexpected
storm—in the body—death a basement we huddle into—in my
workroom, I glue the pages from the calendar over my arms, my legs*

until they are a shell—at first the light so hurt my eyes—my skin felt
peeled back—every touch, every object so close as if inside of me—
nothing now—

I've watched almost everyone I know go there—like sending them on
vacation, remembering the shots my failing eyes took—how the body
becomes not a beach, becomes something with no edges—what could
I recommend? Certainly not this being packed back into something
dying—stuffed into the body like a shoe—

The reporter's report:

The papayas are not more fresh
where the boys unload the wooden
crates, take heavy swings at each other.
And that year I went up to Columbus
And Eliot had said: No-one, no, no-one
knows Lazarus's address, no-one asks
if he comes to work anymore.
And so I went to Chicago
where the snow was just beginning,
and the students jousted at the doorways,
too many suburbs,
and everything cold, seeming cold, after Italy.

And I went to Deerfield, and it was by then 7:30
and long dark, and he and his wife shone through
the window, watching TV behind the remains of dinner—
he and his wife with the images flickering
across their faces, lit behind the window frame
like pieces of a plastic nativity.

I didn't ask for it
Maybe my family prayed
too hard—forcing the screw of prayer

into {God's} flesh until He jumped

Infrequently now, the photo op
me shaking hands with an apostle who afterwards
subtly scrubs his palms with disinfectant
The believers who make the pilgrimage to Chicago
carrying stones or garden gnomes to leave on my lawn
propped against my front door

Silence is the same at night as long ago
when I raise my voice
I cannot more easily rend the sky, the scrim
of what I knew before

Every year he stands at the edge of the river
as the crowd grows on the other side.

He waves sloppily. They stare at him:
diorama of the former life.

He waves and waves in his dreams
while the stone rolls back in front of him.

Note: "To be a mailman is to inhabit this emptiness for hours, to
disturb five hundred abandoned lawns, one after another"
comes from Jonathan Franzen's *How to be Alone.*

I BOUGHT HEMINGWAY'S GHOST A DRINK

I've read the short stories, the novels,
several biographies, so when I saw him
I knew the stage of his life: Not the last
years, but the years before the last years,
years when his belly was big, his arms
spindly, when he was balding and half-
crazy and impotent, when he was a
tiresome asshole, a sad delusional bully,
an increasingly meaner drunk. But
I thought, when will I get a chance
like this again? So I slid onto the stool
next to him at the bar, bought him a
drink. We talked—about baseball, cats,
dogs, fishing. I bought another drink,
told him about that time I was on the
Clark Fork of the Yellowstone, how a
quick hailstorm caught me waist deep
there, how then the sun came out to
limn the clouds golden, how the steep
canyon walls glowed, how the sky
opened up with shafts of sunlight like
angels screaming down, like Manifest
Destiny, like floating Truth revealed,
the sky a glorious Bierstadt painting—
breathing, breathing. How I stood there
shivering amid water hailstones mayflies
trout, gazing up into gauzy gold air—and
the old ghost got excited, said "Yes! Exactly!
I've seen that sky!" I told him I knew he
had, and that I had learned to see it from him.

Scott Wiggerman

MAY

It is the month of bark,
the yard under the sycamore
a shipwreck of shavings
scattered randomly
against the shore of the deck;

the month of exfoliation,
strips of skin sloughed
to the ground in dried-up curls,
when the great tree
becomes blinding white again;

the month when death,
strewn about so beautifully,
can no longer ignore life,
leafing its secrets among the jumble,
the flotsam of mottled browns

and mossy greens,
the former brilliance in shades of gray,
textured with gnarls and knots,
layered like contour maps,
the wild and woody rinds at my feet.

Susan Wood

GRATIFICATION

You're walking through the woods toward Sepiessa Point,
you and the dog, late September, late afternoon, late light
leafing through its book of trees—pitch pine and beetlebung,
scrub oak, the understory all huckleberry like a good plot,
tangled, dark and bittersweet. You're happy enough,
biding your time. Over there, by Tiah's Cove,
some farmer staked his happiness. See,
even his fence extends a foot or two into the water
to keep his goats from drowning. From a high pole,
an osprey jumps feet first into the cove like a kid
jumping off the high board for the first time. And suddenly,
the trees fall off, the sand plain opens up and there it is,
Tisbury Great Pond, and beyond it,
the Atlantic going who knows where, and the water
is an improbable blue, like the blue in the windows
at Chartres, a blue no one has ever been able
to reproduce, but here it is. You can barely see
what keeps them apart, the pond
and the ocean, but there in the distance
is a little strip of beach. And sometimes it wears away,
or someone digs it out, and the ocean
enters the pond at last. In the deep sand,
Cosmo the pug staggers like a happy drunk, charges
the water, eyes the merganser rasping
his old smoker's croak. Every time, arriving here
is a surprise, like getting what you've always wanted
but never thought you'd have—the last piece
of peach pie, all the first editions of your favorite writer—
not to sell, just to keep—that longed-for kiss, someone
knowing, *really knowing,* just how you feel. Now
the sun is going down in flames like a ship
on fire, but slowly, listing a little to the left.
Don't worry, everyone on board gets off.
That's the best part. Everyone is saved.

Susan Wood

In America

Late afternoon, late February in San Diego, the sky a gauze
    bandage
            of blue light, the air
mild, spring-like, and the young black man and I wait for the
    train
            at Seaport Village, just the two of us,
no seaport, no village in sight, just a place for tourists on their
    way
            to other tourist stops, Gas Lamp Quarter
or Old Town, other faux streets of restaurants and galleries,

of T-shirt shops and ye olde lampposts contrived for our
    distraction
            in the Year of Our Lord 2002.
He looks harmless enough in his clean, faded shirt and baggy
    jeans,
            his body soft, doughy,
as though if I touched him my thumbprint would stay visible
            on his flesh forever.
I have friends who know what it is to have a woman

cross to the other side of the street, to be pulled over by cops
    for no reason—
            DWB, they call it, Driving While Black—
but I can't help it, when he asks for a dollar for the train,
    something deep
            in my body turns over,
flops like a hooked fish on a line. He's all dimples and baby
    fat,
            but still, when he opens
the brown paper sack, I imagine a gun in there, a gun black

and thick as his arm, but then I see what he has wrapped up
            in a shiny red box.

He's on his way to the mall in El Cajon where his girlfriend
    works
            nights at Smoothie King, and tonight
he's going to ask her to marry him, he's finally going to do it.
            He points to the Band-aid
on his arm and tells me he sold his blood to pay for the ring

even though he's terrified of needles. First thing next week
    he's going
            to enlist in the Army
if he can pass the test this time. He'll have to lose weight, he
    says,
            but he can do it, and if they get married
now, she can have his benefits. You can see the stars in his
    eyes,
            gold flecks in the deep brown
 that shine in the night sky of his face. In two minutes, I've
    gone from fear

for *my* life to fear for *his* life, and I'm relieved when the train
    ' arrives at last
            because I don't know what to say
about his dreams, which I believe will come to nothing,
    because this is America,
            where the poor stay poor and hope
is not, as Emily Dickinson said, *a thing with feathers*, but is, as
    someone
            once said of the comb-over,
an acceptable convention that doesn't really fool anybody.

Two stops later I'm off with a quick "Good luck" — it's a
    pleasantry
            that seems too little and not right.
He smiles and waves, holds up the ring box for me to see one
    last time,
            and is gone down the tracks.

For months afterward I can't stop wondering what happened
    to him,
        if he got married, joined the Army.
Maybe he got sent to Iraq. Maybe he even died there.

I watch the news each night, thinking I might see him
    somewhere
        among the soldiers in the burning streets.
Of course, I've forgotten exactly what he looked like, though I
    keep trying
        to recall his face, his face like the dark side
of the moon pressed against the window of the swiftly moving
    train.

Susan Wood

THE SOUL BONE

Once I said I didn't have a spiritual bone
in my body and meant by that
I didn't want to think of death,
as though any bone in us
could escape it. Maybe
I was afraid of what I couldn't know
for certain, a thud like the slamming
of a coffin lid, as final and inexplicable
as that. What was the soul anyway,
I wondered, but a homonym for loneliness?
Now, in middle age, or more, I like to imagine it,
the spirit, the soul bone, as though it were hidden
somewhere inside my body, white as a tooth
that falls from a child's mouth, a dove,
the cloud it can fly through. Like bones,
it persists. Little knot of self, stubborn
as wildflowers in a Chilmark field in autumn,
the white ones they call Boneset, for healing,
or the others, Pearly Everlasting.
The rabbis of the *Midrash* believed it and called it
the luz, like the Spanish word for light,
the size of a chickpea or an almond, depending
on which rabbi was telling the story, found,
they said, at the top of the spine or the base,
depending. No one's ever seen it, of course,
but sometimes at night I imagine I can feel it,
shining its light through my body, the bone
luminous, glowing in the dark. Sometimes,
if you listen, you might even hear that light
deep inside me, humming its brave little song.

Adam Zagajewski

DOLPHINS

The sun sets and prying pelicans fly just above the sea's
      smooth skin;
you watch a fisherman killing a caught fish, invincibly
      convinced of his humanity,
while rosy clouds commence their slow, solemn
      march to the night's foothills—
you stay a moment, waiting to see dolphins
—maybe they'll dance their famous, friendly tango once again—
here, on the Gulf of Mexico, where you find tire marks
      and mussels along the broad beaches,
and energetic crabs that exit the sand like workers deserting
      a subterranean factory en masse.
You notice abandoned, rusty loading towers.
You walk along a stone lock and wave to a few anglers,
modest types, fishing not for sport, just in hope
of postponing the last supper.
A vast, brick-red ship from Monrovia sails up
      the port canal
like some bizarre imaginary beast boasting
      of its own oddness,
and briefly blocks the horizon.
You think: it's worth seeking the backwaters, provincial spots
that remember much, but are uncommonly discreet,
quite, humble places, rich, though, in caches,
      hidden pockets of memory
      like hunters' jackets in the fall,
the bustling town's outskirts, wastelands where nothing happens,
      there are no famous actors,
politicians and journalists don't appear,
but sometimes poetry is born in emptiness,
and you start to think that your childhood
      halted here,
here, far from long-familiar streets—

since absence after all can't calculate distance
   in light years or kilometers,
instead it calmly waits for your return, doubtless wondering
   what's become of you. It meets you without fanfare
   and says:
Don't you know me? I'm a stamp from your vanished
   collection,
I'm the stamp that showed you
your first dolphin on a backdrop of unreal, misty blue. I'm
   the sign of travel.
   Unmoving.

      —translated from the Polish by Clare Cavanagh

BIOGRAPHIES AND ACKNOWLEDGMENTS

All poems in this anthology are used with permission of the authors. All rights reserved by the authors. If provided, information regarding previous publication follows each author's biography.

V.T. Abercrombie received Book of the Year 2001 for Poetry award from the North Carolina High Country Writers Association for her chap book *Greatest Hits* (Pudding House Press). Her poems have appeared in literary magazines such as *Roanoke Review, White Rock Review, Bluegrass Literary Review, American Poets & Poetry, Borderlands, Illya 's Honey, Visions International,* and several anthologies, Co-Editor *Christmas in Texas.* She is co-author of *Catering in Houston, Places to Take a Crowd in Houston.*

Carolyn Adams' art, photography, and poetry have appeared in *Sein and Werden, Foliate Oak, The Alembic, Mannequin Envy,* and *Sulphur River Literary Review,* among others. Her e-chapbook *Beautiful Strangers* is available from Lily Press *(Lily Literary Review),* for whom she is currently an Assistant Editor.

James Adams has studied creative writing at the University of Texas, UCLA, and the Université Paris IV *(la Sorbonne).* His poetry has appeared in several anthologies and reviews, including *TimeSlice: Houston Poetry 2005, The David Jones Journal (Wales), The Pebblelake Review,* and *Five Inprint Poets.* Adams' first poetry collection, *Noble Savage* (St. Lukes Presse, 2006) is currently nominated for a 2007 Pulitzer Prize. Several of his poems have also been nominated for a 2007 Pushcart Prize.

Alan Ainsworth's work has appeared in *The Atlantic Monthly, The Paris Review, The American Book Review, The New England Review,*

ArtLies, and elsewhere. He edited *75 Arguments,* a reader, for McGraw-Hill. He is currently chair of English at Houston Community College Central.

Mike Alexander lives in Houston with wife and fellow-poet K. A. Thomas. He moderates an on-line sonnet workshop. His work has appeared in Mutabilis Press' *TimeSlice,* Parallel Press' *Fashioned Pleasures, Alabama Literary Review, New Orleans Review, Texas Review, Link, Avatar,* and other publications.

"Charybdis" appeared in *Znine.*

Barry Ballard's poetry has most recently appeared in *Prairie Schooner, The Connecticut Review, Margie,* and *Puerto del Sol.* His most recent collection is *A Body Speaks Through Fence Lines* (Pudding House, 2006). He writes from Burleson, Texas.

Alicia Bankston is an Associate Professor of English at Montgomery College in Conroe, Texas, and a member of the Montgomery County Literary Arts Council. Her poems have been published in *Switched-on Gutenberg, Labyrinth,* and *Jeopardy,* and she has held various editorial positions on literary magazines including *The Bellingham Review.*

Wendy Barker has published four collections of poems and two chapbooks. Recipient of NEA and Rockefeller fellowships, as well as the Mary Elinore Smith Award from the editors of *The American Scholar,* she has had poems appear in such journals as *Boulevard, Ontario Review, The Journal, Poetry,* and *North American Review.* She is Poet in Residence and a professor of English at the University of Texas at San Antonio.

Joe Barnes is a three-time juried poet at the Houston Poetry Fest. His work has appeared in *Time Slice: Houston Poetry 2005,* an anthology of Houston poets, *Measure, Spiky Palm,* and *Illya's Honey.* He is a past finalist in the Howard Nemerov national sonnet competition. Barnes is also a playwright.

David Bart is assistant editor for *Illya's Honey,* the quarterly journal of the Dallas Poets Community. His poems have previously appeared in *Borderlands: Texas Poetry Review.*

Kristi Beer works for Inprint, a literary non-profit organization in Houston, and was a juried poet at the 2003 and 2006 Houston Poetry Fest. She has had poetry published in *TimeSlice, Frogpond* and *Happy*. She lives in Bellaire with her daughter, a much younger version of herself, and four cats.

Ann Reisfeld Boutté was a juried poet in the Houston Poetry Fest in 2001 and 2005. She is a former feature writer for a national wire service. Her work has appeared in *New Texas*, five *Texas Poetry Calendars, Bylines Writer's Desk Calendar 2006, Suddenly V, Houston Woman Magazine*, and other publications. Boutté has an M.A. in Journalism from The American University.

Carolyn Praytor Boyd's work has appeared in UH-CL *Bayousphere, The Limestone Circle, Bellowing Ark, Edgar, Atlanta Review, Writers' Digest, Swirl, 2006 Round Top Anthology, Broken Bridge Review, Words-myth* and *TimeSlice: Houston Poetry 2005*. She was a juried poet for Houston Poetry Fest 2006.

Stella Brice received her degree in English Literature from Rice University; and has worked, variously, as housecleaner, tarot reader and performance artist. Her writing has appeared or is forthcoming in *Frank, Fine Madness, Southern Poetry Review*, the anthology of border poetry *Tierra Cruzada/Crossed Land* and many others. She is a winner of the John Z. Bennet Prize and is co-editor of the literary journal *Art Club*. Her first collection of poems, *Green Lion*, was released in the spring of 2005.

Jericho Brown's poems have appeared or are forthcoming in *Prairie Schooner, AGNI, and Post Road*. He holds a Ph.D. in Creative Writing and Literature from the University of Houston and an M.F.A. from the University of New Orleans, and currently serves as poetry editor of *Gulf Coast: A Journal of Literature and Fine Arts*.

"Prayer of the Backhanded" appeared in *New England Review*; "Like Father" appeared in *Callaloo*. Both poems are from *Please*, currently a finalist manuscript for the 2007 New Issues Poetry Prize. The manuscript was also chosen by Terrance Hayes as runner-up for the 2006 AWP Donald Hall Award.

Robert Burlingame is a graduate of the University of New Mexico, Brown (Ph. D.), and Fulbright Scholar, Queen Mary College, University of London. He taught in the graduate school at the University of Texas (El Paso) and has published poems in *Texas Observer, Southwest Review, Pushcart Prize, South Dakota Review, Kansas Quarterly, Massachusetts Review*, and many others. Burlingame lives on a ranch in West Texas with his wife Linda, an artist.

Joseph Campana is the author of *The Book of Faces* (Graywolf, 2005). His poems appear in *Beloit Poetry Journal, Hotel Amerika, New England Review, Gulf Coast, Prairie Schooner, Poetry*, and *TriQuarterly*, and are forthcoming in *Conjunctions, Kenyon Review, Subtropics, Field, Green Court, Cincinnati Review*, and elsewhere. He is the recipient of a 2007 Creative Writing Fellowship in Poetry from the NEA. Currently, he is completing a book of poems called *Sheltering Bough*. He teaches Renaissance literature and creative writing at Rice University.

Native Texan, **Mary Margaret Carlisle** is the founder of PST's Gulf Coast Poets, Executive Director of Sol Magazine's Projects, Ampersand Poetry Journal Editor, and a Poetry Society of Texas Councilor. Recent works appeared in *TimeSlice, Bayousphere, Texas Poetry Calendar, HPF Anthology, Mountain Time*, and *In the Yard*. http://sol-magazine.org

Cyrus Cassells is the author of four acclaimed books of poetry: *The Mud Actor, Soul Make a Path Through Shouting, Beautiful Signor*, and *More Than Peace and Cypresses*. His fifth book, *The Crossed-Out Swastika*, is forthcoming. Among his honors are a Lannan Literary Award, a William Carlos Williams Award, a Pushcart Prize, two NEA grants, and a Lambda Literary Award. He is a tenured Associate Professor of English at Texas State University-San Marcos, and lives in Austin and Paris.

R. T. Castleberry is an assistant editor at *Lily Literary Review*, the former co-editor/co-publisher of the poetry monthly, *Curbside Review* and a co-founder/director of The Flying Dutchman Writers Troupe. His work has appeared in numerous journals including *Green Mountains Review, The Alembic, Texas Review, Concho River Review, Poet Lore, Common Ground Review* and *Pacific Review*.

D. B. Cherry received a Glenn C. Cambor / Inprint fellowship to attend the University of Houston Creative Writing Program. As an undergraduate, he was awarded the Sylvan Karchmer Prize for Fiction and the Howard Moss Prize for Poetry. He lives in Houston with his wife and daughter.

Dr. **Mary Cimarolli**, retired professor of English at Richland College, Dallas, Texas, has published poems in several anthologies and literary journals. Her memoir, *The Bootlegger's Other Daughter* (Texas A&M University Press, 2003), was chosen as one of three finalists in 2004 for the PEN/Martha Albrand Award for the Art of the Memoir.

Sandra Cisneros is the author of three volumes of poetry: *Bad Boys*, 1980; *My Wicked Wicked Ways*, 1987; and *Loose Woman*, 1994, in addition to short stories, novels and essays. In 1995 Cisneros was awarded the MacArthur Foundation Fellowship. Most recently she was awarded the Texas Medal of the Arts, 2003. She has worked as a teacher, a poet-in-the-schools, and as a visiting writer at a number of universities across the country. Cisneros lives in San Antonio with her partner, a filmmaker, and several animals, little and large.

Kathleen Cook is a life-long admirer of the possibilities of language. She is an instructor of English-as-a-Second-Language and German. For many years, Houston has been her home. South Texas, the Hill Country, and the Coastal Plains are backdrops to her poetry.

Sarah Cortez is a poet and a police officer. Her first volume of poetry *How To Undress A Cop* was published in 2000 and contains the poems which won her the 1999 PEN Texas Literary Award in Poetry. She has recently edited an anthology of short memoir by young Latinos across the U.S. entitled *Windows into My World: Latino Youth Write Their Lives*. (Arte Publico Press, 2007).

Maryke Cramerus is a psychotherapist practicing in Houston, Texas. She has published articles on trauma, self-distancing and self-disavowing, and has a poem published in *Poetry Midwest*

Stan Crawford lives in the Heights in Houston, Texas with his wife Dawn, their cat Kismet and dysfunctional Chow-Labrador mix Java. He practices civil trial law when not writing poetry. His poems have been published in *Poet Lore, The Comstock Review, Borderlands: Texas Poetry Review,* and *Water-Stone Review,* among other journals, and he was a juried poet in the Houston Poetry Fest 2003.

Carolyn Dahl's poems have been published in *Sojourn, TimeSlice, Suddenly, Echoes for a New Room, The Texas Poetry Calendars,* and the coming *2008 Women Artists' Datebook.* She has been a juried poet twice and a juror for the Houston Poetry Fest. Also an artist, she writes for textile magazines, has appeared on Home and Garden Television and PBS, and is the author of two books: *Natural Impressions* (Watson-Guptill Publications) and *Transforming Fabric* (Krause Publications).

André de Korvin was born in Berlin, Germany from Russian parents, and raised in Paris, France. Studied math at the Sorbonne and graduated with a Ph.D. in mathematics from UCLA. His first book of poems *The Four Hard Edges Of War* came out in 1992. His second book of poems *Dreaming Indigo Time* has been published in 2005 by Sulphur River Press.

Ysabel de la Rosa is a fourth-generation native Texan whose feature writing and poetry have appeared or are forthcoming in numerous publications in the U.S. and Spain, including *Calyx, Nimrod, Oregon East,* and *Southwest American Literature.* She was a finalist for the 2006 Pablo Neruda Poetry Award. She lives in Wichita Falls.

Carol Denson writes poems and essays, often about the pleasures of being the mom of her nine-year-old son. She teaches second grade, is a very proficient sleeper, is very grateful there's water in the creek behind the house, and loves to contra dance. She lives in Austin.

Marco A. Domínguez currently resides in Lubbock, Texas, where he is working on his Ph. D. at Texas Tech University. He is an assistant poetry editor for both *32 Poems* and *Iron Horse Literary Review* and his poetry has appeared in *DIAGRAM, Indiana Review, Rattle, Willow Springs*, and elsewhere.

"The Blue Jay" appeared in *Indiana Review*.

KB Eckhardt wonders if readers really want authors to be stripped of mystery in these sketches. To comply, Eckhardt reveals that he/she is in possession of at least one graduate degree, more than a single publication credit and evidence attesting to the existence of said being. Exposed.

B. H. Fairchild has been recipient of Guggenheim, Rockefeller, and NEA Fellowhips. His third book of poems, *The Art of the Lathe*, was a Finalist for the National Book Award and received the Kingsley Tufts Poetry Award and the William Carlos Williams Award. *Early Occult Memory Systems of the Lower Midwest*, his fourth book, received the National Book Critics Circle Award and the Bobbitt Prize from the Library of Congress.

Carolyn Tourney Florek is a poet, visual artist, and publisher who lives in Houston, Texas with her family. She is the co-founder of Mutabilis Press, a non-profit literary press, and editor of *TimeSlice: Houston Poetry 2005*. Her poetry has been published in *Illya's Honey, Green Hills Literary Lantern*, the Houston Poetry Fest anthology, and other publications.

Larry L. Fontenot makes his home in Sugar Land, Texas. He has had poetry published in *Arrowsmith, Boxcar Poetry Review, Curbside Review, i.e. magazine, Pebble Lake Review, Red River Review, Shit Creek Review* and *Sulphur River Literary Review*. Larry was a featured poet at the 2000 Houston Poetry Fest. A chapbook, *Choices & Consequences*, was the winner of the Maverick Press 1996 Southwest Poets' Series Chapbook competition.

Priscilla Frake's poems have appeared or are forthcoming in many literary publications in the U.S., including *Nimrod, Atlanta Review, The Midwest Quarterly, The Spoon River Poetry Review, The Sun* and journals in Great Britain and Ireland including: *The New Welsh Review, Cutting Teeth, Orbis, Cyphers,* and *Deliberately Thirsty*. Her chapbook, *Argument Against Winter*, was published by Cloud in the U.K. A former geologist, she now makes jewelry and poems in the Houston area.

Adamarie Fuller is a native Houstonian, graduate of Milby High School and Stephen F. Austin University. Fuller is a CPA employed as the Assistant Treasurer and Accounting Manager of Mitsui Tubular Products. She has two children, both in Austin; daughter Rebecca, a realtor, and son Stephen, a starving artist/musician, are very happy in their chosen endeavors.

Edwin Gallaher's poems have appeared in *The Paris Review* and are anthologized in *Retellings: a Thematic Literature Anthology*.

Jeannie Gambill lives in Bellaire, Texas. Her poetry has appeared in *Gulf Coast*, and she has been a finalist in the Ruth G. Hardman/ Nimrod Poetry Competition.

Lewis Garvin has taught at the College of William and Mary, the University of New Orleans, Metairie Park Country Day, and in Fort Bend. He has published in *Spiky Palm* and *New Orleans Review*.

Denton resident **Wayne Lee Gay** holds degrees in music history and musicology, and is currently enrolled in the graduate program in creative writing at the University of North Texas. In a previous career as a journalist, he was finalist for the Pulitzer Prize for criticism.

John Gorman lives in Galveston and teaches literature and creative writing at the University of Houston-Clear Lake. His work, gathered in three chapbooks, has appeared in *TimeSlice* and many other publications in Texas, nationally, and in Canada.

Jennifer Grotz was born in Canyon, Texas. Now she lives in North Carolina, where she teaches at the University of North Carolina at Greensboro and in the Warren Wilson MFA Program.

"Alchemy" and "The Woodstove" appeared in *New England Review*.

Laurie A. Guerrero's poetry has appeared in *Voices Along the River, Literary Mama, The Texas Poetry Calendar 2007* and is forthcoming in *The Palo Alto Review* and *The Texas Poetry Calendar 2008*. Two-time winner of the Rosemary Thomas Poetry Prize, her chapbook manuscript was a finalist in a competition sponsored by Kulupi Press. Though born and raised in San Antonio, she is currently an Ada Comstock Scholar at Smith College in Northampton, Massachusetts, where she lives with her husband and three children.

William F. Guest, a resident of Houston, Texas, recently retired as Chairman of a life insurance holding company. Previously, he practiced law in Houston for about 25 years. Poetry has been a life long interest. A few poems have been published in poetry journals, but no submissions have been made in recent years. One poem was selected for the Houston Poetry Fest a few years ago. Mr. Guest has attended several Inprint Poetry Workshops.

Laura Quinn Guidry's poetry has been published in *The Texas Review, Concho River Review, Louisiana Literature, Earth's Daughters, Texas Poetry Calendars 2003* and *2007* and in the recent anthology *In the Eye*. She lives in Houston and Carmine, Texas.

A native Texan, **Michelle Hartman** is a book reviewer for the University of North Texas Press and recently finished a Political Science-Pre Law Bachelors degree at TWU. Her poems have appeared in *Sojourn, Illya's Honey, Red River Review, The Texas Review,* and *descant,* and received Honorable Mention in the Dallas Poets Community 2006 national poetry contest. Her fictional account of Fort Worth history, *They Were Dead When I Met Them*, is currently crawling over various transoms in New York.

Kurt Heinzelman co-founded and for ten years edited the award-winning journal, *The Poetry Miscellany*; he is currently Advisory Editor for the *Bat City Review*. A multiple nominee for the Pushcart Prize Anthology, his two books of poetry, *The Halfway Tree* (2000) and *Black Butterflies* (2004) were both finalists for the Natalie Ornish Award. He is a professor of English at the University of Texas.

Jesse G. Herrera is a XXX shot of tequila like the late, great Chicano poet, Trinidad Sanchez Jr. with a Charles Bukowski chaser, straight up, stone sober. He was born en San Anto, Tejas pero soy de Laredo, Tejas.

Grady Hillman is a well-published poet, literary translator (Spanish, Russian and Quechua), folklorist and essayist. He is the author of two volumes of poetry (*Razor Wire* received the Austin Book Award in 1986) and a book of Quechua Inca translations, *Return of the Inca*. He lives in Austin.

Edward Hirsch, president of the John Simon Guggenheim Memorial Foundation, taught at the University of Houston for eighteen years.

"The Minimalist Museum" appeared in *Per Contra*; "Branch Library" appeared in *Poetry*; "Krakow, 6 a.m." appeared in *Five Points*.

Tony Hoagland has published three collections of poetry: *Sweet Ruin, Donkey Gospel* and *What Narcissism Means To Me*. He teaches at the University of Houston.

"I Have News for You" and "Nature" appeared in *The American Poetry Review*; "Texaco" appeared in *The Threepenny Review*.

Ann Howells serves on the board of Dallas Poets Community—NPC and is editor of its journal, *Illya 's Honey*. She was named a "distinguished poet of Dallas" by the Dallas Library in 2001, and in 2004, was nominated for a Pushcart. Her work appears in many small journals including: *Borderlands, Gertrude, Sulphur River Review, Concho River Review, Sentence* and several anthologies.

"Initiating My Daughter" appeared in the anthology *Blood Offerings*, published by Incarnate Muse Press.

Robb Jackson was born and raised in Ohio, where he spent much of his time growing up exploring the water, beaches, coves and swamps along Lake Erie. He's gone to school a lot, and he's enjoyed a number of different jobs, but nineteen years ago he exchanged his sweet water origins for a saltwater life on the coastal bend of the Gulf of Mexico in south Texas where he writes and teaches at Texas A&M University-Corpus Christi.

Ken Jones has been a published poet for over 20 years in academic and underground journals, magazines, anthologies, websites and other forums. He earned an M.A. in English/Creative Writing from the University of Texas at Austin and is a full-time faculty member at The Art Institute of Houston. He has also given readings of his work at innumerable bookstores, bars, coffeehouses, conferences and other forums. His collection of poems *Unutterable Blunders and Palace Disasters* was released by PlainView Press in 2006

Melanie Jordan was raised in Middle Tennessee, though she currently lives and works in Houston, Texas. Her work has appeared in or is forthcoming in *Iowa Review, Third Coast, Southeast Review, Crab Orchard Review*, and others. She was recently an editor for *Gulf Coast* and *Lyric Poetry Review*, and would love to edit another journal soon. She teaches for the Houston Community College and the University of Houston. Her manuscript, *The Broken Zoo*, was a finalist for Switchback Books' 2007 Gatewood Prize.

Claire Kageyama-Ramakrishnan received an M.F.A. in poetry from the University of Virginia, and an M.A. in literature from the University of California at Berkeley. At the University of Houston she was a Cambor Fellow and earned a Ph.D. in literature and creative writing. In 2006 her poetry manuscript was selected by Kimiko Hahn for the Four Way Books 2006 Intro Prize in Poetry. She works as a full-time instructor at Houston Community College. She lives in Houston with her husband, Raj and their three cats.

"Owens Valley, 1942" and "The Moon and Kaguya" will be included in *Shadow Mountain*, copyright © 2008 by Claire Kageyama-Ramakrishnan, to be published by Four Way Books.

Sharon Klander's poems have appeared in numerous publications, including *The New Republic, Kansas Quarterly, Shenandoah, and New Letters*, and in anthologies, including *The Writing Room* and *The Art and Craft of Poetry*. In addition, her poetry was judged 1st Place in the 1998 New Letters Literary Awards and 2nd Place in the 2001 American Literary Review Competition. Her published scholarship concerns the poetry of John Haines and Colette Inez. She teaches at Houston Community College.

"Grief Song" initially appeared as "Three Deaths" in *Calypso: Journal of Narrative Poetry and Poetic Fiction*.

Jacqueline Kolosov's poetry collection is *Vago* (Lewis-Clark, 2007). *Modigliani's Muse* is forthcoming (WordTech). Her young adult novel is *The Red Queen's Daughter* (Hyperion, 2007). She is on the creative writing faculty at Texas Tech.

Judith Kroll, author of two collections of poetry, has also published poems *in Poetry, The New Yorker,* and *Southern Review,* and a critical book on Sylvia Plath. Her creative nonfiction has been published in journals including *Kenyon Review, Southwest Review,* and *River City.* Recipient of two National Endowment for the Arts fellowships in poetry, Kroll has been awarded other grants for creative nonfiction and for translating South Indian mystical poems. She is on the Creative Writing faculty of The University of Texas at Austin.

Laurie Clements Lambeth's first collection of poetry, *Veil and Burn,* was selected by Maxine Kumin for the 2006 National Poetry Series Open Competition. A PhD and MFA graduate of the University of Houston, her poems and essays have appeared in *The Paris Review, Indiana Review, Mid-American Review, The Iowa Review,* and elsewhere. She lives in Houston.

Erica Lehrer is a poet, journalist and founding member of Net Poets Society (NetPoSo), a Houston-based poets' group. Her writing has appeared in both national and regional publications. A graduate of Princeton University (BA, English) and N.Y.U. Law School, she never thought she'd be living in Texas. However, she's loving it!

Rich Levy is a poet and (since 1995) executive director of Inprint, a nonprofit literary arts organization in Houston. He earned his MFA at the Iowa Writers Workshop, and his poems have appeared in *Boulevard, Gulf Coast, Pool, The Texas Observer,* and elsewhere. A jazz obsessive, he and his wife have three children, two dogs, and one sleepy cat.

Michael Lieberman has published four collections of poetry. His new book, *Far-From-Equilibrium Conditions,* will be published in

November 2007, and won the Texas Review Poetry Prize for 2007. He is a research physician who lives with his wife Susan in Houston.

Inspired by an Inprint workshop, **Thad Logan** has recently completed an MFA in creative writing at Warren Wilson College. For the past twenty years, she has been teaching in the English Department at Rice University, specializing in Victorian Studies. She and her husband live in Houston, with their daughter and other animals.

Robert Lunday is the author of one book of poetry, *Mad Flights* (Ashland Poetry Press, 2001). He is currently finishing a memoir, *Fayettenam*, based on his father's letters home from Vietnam in 1969.

Peggy Zuleika Lynch has a BS from UT, Austin, and an MFA (highest honors) from SMU, Dallas. She was short listed for Poet Laureate of Texas for 2007/2008, and has been nominated for five Pushcart Prizes.

Cynthia Macdonald founded the Creative Writing Program at the University of Houston in 1979. She has published six collections of poems, *Amputations, Transplants, (W)holes, Alternate Means of Transport, Living Wills* and *I Can't Remember*. Her grants and awards include an NEA grant, a Guggenheim Fellowship, and a National Academy and Institute of Art and letters Award in recognition of her achievement in poetry. Retired from teaching, she lives in Houston, Texas.

> "And Cause His Countenance to Shine Upon You" and "Two Brothers in a Field of Absence" from *Living Wills, New and Selected Poems*, copyright © 1991 by Cynthia Macdonald, published by Alfred A. Knopf.

Dodie Messer Meeks has poetry in a couple of hundred literary quarterlies and a couple of murder mysteries available on Amazon.com. She's working on a novel set in Galveston in the fifties. An illustrated collection of her poetry entitled, *When I Got Dressed Again*, published by the Arts Alliance in Clear Lake City, has sold out.

John R. Milkereit has been writing for several years and was juried poet at the 2007 Austin International Poetry Festival and will be published in *Swirl* later. He recently completed two Inprint poetry workshops while holding down his day job as a salesperson. He owns an ivy plant and some fake fish.

Laura Elizabeth Miller is a dancer, poet, and new mother.

Carolina Monsiváis is a recipient of the Premio Poesía Tejana for her book, *Somewhere Between Houston and El Paso: Testimonies of a Poet* (Wings Press). A dedicated advocate/activist in the field of violence against women and children, Monsiváis co-founded The Women Writers' Collective. She completed her M.F.A. in poetry at New Mexico State University, and she resides in her hometown, El Paso, Texas.

Jack Myers, the 2003 Poet Laureate of Texas, is the author of seventeen books of and about poetry including *The Portable Poetry Workshop* (Thomson/Wadsworth, 2004) and *The Glowing River: New & Selected Poems* (Invisible Cities Press, 2001). He has been the recipient of two National Endowment for the Arts Fellowships and is a National Poetry Series Open Competition winner. He is former Director of creative writing at Southern Methodist Univ. and current president of The Writer's Garrett, a Dallas literary center.

Naomi Shihab Nye is author/editor of more than 25 books of poetry and prose, has worked widely as a visiting writer for many years, and lives in old downtown San Antonio with her photographer husband, Michael Nye.

Having never been "discovered," **Monica Teresa Ortiz** nevertheless still writes poetry, flash fiction, and novels [simultaneously beginning but never finishing] in her spare time. She holds a BA from UT

Austin, an MFA from UTEP and grew up on a line of land somewhere between Amarillo and Lubbock.

"Enlistment Papers" appeared in *Palabra: A Magazine of Chicano and Latino Literary Art*.

Mary Gomez Parham has published poems in the *The Caribbean Writer*, *The Atlanta Review* and other literary magazines and anthologies, as well as the *Texas Poetry Calendar*. Her scholarly essays on Latin American literature have appeared in many journals and books in the U.S. and Latin America.

Dave Parsons' first collection of poems, *Editing Sky*, was the winner of the 1999 Texas Review Poetry Prize and a 2000 Finalist for the Violet Crown Book Awards. His second book, *Color of Mourning*, was released from Texas Review Press/Texas A&M University Press in 2007.

"Austin Relativity" and "Orange County April 29, 2005" from *Color of Mourning*, copyright © 2007 by Dave Parsons, published by Texas Review Press.

Emmy Pérez is the author of *Solstice* (Swan Scythe Press, 2003) and her work appears in *The Wind Shifts: New Latino Poetry* (University of Arizona Press, 2007). She has received poetry fellowships from the Fine Arts Work Center in Provincetown and the New York Foundation for the Arts. Currently, she teaches in the MFA program at the University of Texas-Pan American.

"It's Pouring" appeared in *The Wind Shifts: The New Latino Poetry;* "Midnight Rooster Song" appeared in *The Laurel Review*.

Donna Perkins is a visual artist who writes in fits and spurts. Her writings include: *TimeSlice, Houston Poetry 2005*, University of Houston's New Playwrights Workshop productions 2005 ("Bed") and 2003 ("Touching Leaves"). Donna is the co-founder and current facilitator of The Archway Readings which recently celebrated it's 10th anniversary.

Jere Pfister has had several of her plays performed locally and has experimented with writing for musical theatre as well as dance. She has worked as a mentor in the Alley Theatre's Houston Young Playwright's Exchange. She performed as a storyteller for some years and is currently working on a memoir.

Robert Phillips is the author of several books of poetry, including *Circumstances Beyond Our Control, Spinach Days* and *Breakdown Lane,* which was named a Notable Book of the Year by the *New York Times Book Review* and was also a runner-up for the Poets' Prize. His honors include the Award in Literature from the American Academy of Arts and Letters. He teaches at the University of Houston, where he has been director of the Creative Writing Program and now is a John and Rebecca Moores Scholar.

> "Triangle Shirtwaist Factory Fire" from *Circumstances Beyond Our Control,* copyright © 2006 by Robert Phillips, published by Johns Hopkins University Press.

John Poch directs the creative writing program at Texas Tech. His first book, *Poems,* is published with Orchises Press. He is the editor of *32 Poems Magazine.*

Deseree Marie Probasco is a graduate of Princeton University with a degree in Literature, concentrating in avant-garde poetry. She resides in Conroe with her husband Daniel, and daughter Isabel, a crazy dog, and two goats. She is working on her first book length collection of poetry and artwork.

Barbara Ras is the author of *Bite Every Sorrow,* which won the Walt Whitman Award and the Kate Tufts Discovery Award, and *One Hidden Stuff.* Her poems have appeared in *TriQuarterly, Massachusetts Review, The New Yorker, Gulf Coast, Orion,* and other anthologies and magazines nationwide. She has taught in the Warren Wilson MFA Program for Writers and directs Trinity University Press in San Antonio.

> "Big Bull and Little Dog" and "Moonshine" from *One Hidden Stuff,* copyright © 2006 by Barbara Ras. Used by permission of Penguin, a division of Penguin Group (USA).

Robin Reagler writes poems and essays in Houston, where she is the Executive Director of Writers in the Schools (WITS). Her poetry has appeared in *Ploughshares, VOLT, American Letters and Commentary, Gulf Coast,* and other journals.

"The Grief Snapshot" appeared in *Lyric.*

Daniel Rice has his degree in English Literature, *Summa Cum Laude,* from the University of Houston and a Doctor of Jurisprudence from its law school. He hosts the popular poetry reading series at The Woodlands Barnes & Noble. Daniel is a published poet, an award winning playwright and writes fiction.

Born in Galveston in 1941, **John E. Rice** is a writer of poetry, fiction and non-fiction and an artist working in several media. Rice has worked in medical research, horticulture and international shipping. He is an executive in the international maritime industry and is married with four children and four grandchildren.

Sally Ridgway's poetry has been published in literary journals such as Gulf *Coast, Texas Review* and *Sulphur River Literary Review.* She has led creative writing workshops, taught English at high schools in Galveston and Houston and at Houston Community College, and has an MFA in Writing from Vermont College.

Daniel Rifenburgh's first book, *Advent,* was published in 2002 by the Waywiser Press of London and received the Natalie Ornish Award from the Texas Institute of Letters. In 1996 he received the Robert H. Winner Award from the Poetry Society of America. He holds an M.A. from the University of Florida and has lived in Houston since 1988. In 2005 he enjoyed a Dobie Paisano Fellowship from the University of Texas and the Texas Institute of Letters.

Erika Rodriguez Hernandez is a college freshman at Westminster College in Salt Lake City, UT where she is working towards a B.A. in English. She was a juried poet for Houston Poetry Fest 2006 and won the National Scholastic American Voices Award last year. Her hobbies include college.

Iris Rozencwajg grew up in Aruba. Introduced to poetry writing in Inprint workshops, she is enrolled in Vermont College's MFA program while continuing to teach English at Houston Community College.

Paul Ruffin is Regents Distinguished Professor of English at Sam Houston State University, where he edits *The Texas Review* and directs Texas Review Press. His published works include two novels, three collections of short stories, five collections of poetry, two books of essays, and eleven other books that he edited or coedited.

"Burying" appeared in the *Alaska Quarterly Review;* "Llano Estacado: The Naming" appeared in *Midwest Quarterly.*

Benjamin Alire Sáenz, novelist and poet, makes his home on the border. His latest book of poems, *Dreaming the End of War*, was published by Copper Canyon Press. His fifth novel, *Names on a Map*, will be published by Harper Perennial in February of 2008. He is currently working on a new book of poems, *What Remains of a Life.*

M. Duncan Scheps has lived in Texas since 1970 (currently Houston). She is a writer, wildlife rehabilitator, and theatrical costumer to name a few crazily unrelated pursuits. Her poetry has appeared in *LIGHT Quarterly, Sacred Journey, NutHouse,* and *miller's pond.* She lives with her husband and Cleo, a spotty dog.

Kate Schmitt is a poet whose writing has been published in anthologies including *Earth Shattering Poems, Roots and Flowers,* and *Light Gathering Poems*, as well as in literary journals. She has a creative writing and visual arts degree from Colgate University and received her M.F.A. from University of Houston's Creative Writing Program where she is currently completing a Ph.D. She teaches literature and writing at University of Houston and Inprint, Inc.

Varsha Shah's poems have appeared in *Between Heaven And Texas* by Wyman Meinzer, a University of Texas book of photography & poetry, *Time Slice, Texas Observer, Borderlands, Five Inprint Poets,* and *Convergence* among others. She enjoys reading translated works of Latin American, European poets and Eastern poets as well as contemporary American poetry. She continues to write poetry in her mother tongue, Gujarati. A first-generation Indian-American, Varsha is a financial professional and lives in Houston, Texas.

ire'ne lara silva lives in Austin, Texas and is the Executive Coordinator for the Macondo Writing Workshop. Her poetry has appeared in various journals and anthologies, including *The Worcester*

Review, Rhapsoidia, Soleado: Revista de Literatura y Cultura, Borderlands: Texas Poetry Review, Sin Fronteras/Writers Without Borders, Palabra, The Mesquite Review, Cantos al Sexto Sol Anthology, and *the 2001 AIPF diverse city odyssey* anthology.

Eva Skrande graduated from Sarah Lawrence College, Iowa, and The University of Houston. Her book, *My Mother's Cuba,* (River City Poetry Series) will be published in the spring of 2008. Skrande lives in Houston with her husband and daughter and teaches at the University of Houston-Downtown and the High School for the Performing and Visual Arts.

Larue Smith is a native of Huntsville, Texas. She attended Sam Houston State University where she studied creative writing under Jewel Gibson and later audited classes under Paul Ruffin. She has traveled through all seven continents and brings a sense of place to her poetry not only from exotic locales but regionally as well. She has published poetry in *ByLine, Poetry at Roundtop, Panhandle, Threshold,* and various other publications.

Loueva Smith's poetry has been published in *DoubleTake, The Texas Review, Kalliope, Curbside Review,* and *Impetus.* Her poetry has been Published in the anthologies: *TimeSlice,* and *Houston Poetry Fest 2001 and 2002.* She was the featured poet at the Houston Poetry Fest in 2001 and 2002.

Allison Smythe recently moved to Missouri after spending 29 of her years in Dallas, Lubbock and Houston. Recent work has appeared in *Cranky, Versal V, Verse Daily, The Southern Review, The Gettysburg Review* and elsewhere. She and husband, Wayne Leal, continue to maintain their Houston graphic design firm virtually from Rocheport.

Michael Sofranko is a poet, writer, and editor whose most recent book, American Sign, received the 2003 Antonio Machado Prize in Poetry. He teaches Creative Writing at Cambridge University, England, as part of the Oxbridge Summer Studies Program, and is a faculty member at Houston Community College - Northwest. An avid tennis player and basketball fan, he is currently writing *Voices Without Borders,* an anthology of works related to the subject of immigration

Rebecca Spears is a poet and essayist, who teaches Creative Writing for SMU Continuing Education. Her poetry has appeared in *Comstock Review, Natural Bridge, Nimrod, Calyx, Sentence, Minnesota Review, Dos Passos Review, Texas Review,* and *Borderlands,* and in the anthologies *Texas in Poetry 2* and *Cyber-Collection: The Bennington Writers Collective.*

Sandi Stromberg's poetry has appeared in *TimeSlice: Houston Poetry 2005, Illya's Honey, Curbside Review, Suddenly V, NEWN* and several anthologies. She was a juried poet in the Houston Poetry Fest in 2004 and 2006. Her translations of Dutch poetry have been published in the United States, the Netherlands and Luxembourg.

Carmen Tafolla, a native of San Antonio, is the author of five books of poetry and numerous short stories, screenplays, children's works and essays, including the award-winning poetry collection *Sonnets to Human Beings.* Winner of the 1999 Art of Peace Award, Tafolla has presented hundreds of performances and readings throughout the US and in Europe, Mexico, Canada, and New Zealand.

"*Curandera*, Healer" and "Feeding You" appeared in *The Langdon Review of the Arts in Texas.*

Jessica Tarrand is a native of Houston. She graduated from St. Mary's College with a B.A. in English. She has worked as a tutor, a legal secretary, and a pet sitter. She is currently employed at an insurance company, where she spends most of the day writing on yellow pads of legal paper.

Larry D. Thomas, 2008 Texas Poet Laureate, has published seven collections of poems, and has two additional collections in press: *The Fraternity of Oblivion* (Timberline Press, Fall 2007) and *New and Selected Poems* (TCU Press, Spring 2008).

Stephanie B. Thome was born and raised in El Paso, Texas. She is currently living in Lubbock, and attending Texas Tech University where she will receive her PhD in December 2007. Stephanie writes about the Chicana experience in Texas, specifically the theme of love and the blurred borders of romance, dreams, and reality.

Gail Tirone is originally from New York City. She has lived in Asia, Europe and the Caribbean. She has a B.A. from Princeton University and M.A. from the University of Houston. Her poetry has appeared in *Free China Review, Houston Poetry Fest Anthologies 1993* and *1994, i.e. magazine, The Nassau Literary Review, Sulphur River Review*, and elsewhere.

William Turner has been a geologist since 1961 and resided and worked in Houston for the past 23 years. He has been writing poetry for most of that time. It has been for his own edification. From 1961 to 1964 he was on the faculty of the University of Kentucky and again from 1969 to 1975. While he is a lover of the earth, his current interests include the study of C.G. Jung's writings and the art, literature and history of the western world.

Evangelina Vigil-Piñón is the author of three books of poetry and a bilingual children's book. She is a recipient of numerous literary awards, including an NEA Fellowship for Creative Writers. She is also the translator of Tomás Rivera's, *Y No Se Lo Tragó la Tierra/And the Earth Did Not Devour Him*, and a contributing editor of *Woman of Her Word: Hispanic Women Write*. A native of San Antonio, Vigil-Piñón resides in Houston where she works as a TV producer.

Randall Watson is the author of two books of poetry and one of fiction. *Las Delaciones del Sueño* is published by the Universidad Veracruzana in Xalapa, Mexico, and *The Sleep Accusations* was the recipient of the 2004 Blue Lynx Prize in Poetry at Eastern Washington University Press. *Petals*, winner of the 2006-07 Quarterly West Novella Competition, is published under the pseudonym Ellis Reece.

"Perishables" appeared in *Chelsea*.

Sasha West's poetry and reviews have appeared or are forthcoming in *American Letters & Commentary, The Canary, Pebble Lake Review, Third Coast, Margie, Born, Chelsea, American Poet*, and *Ninth Letter*. Her work has been nominated for a Pushcart prize. She received her doctorate from the University of Houston, where she was the managing editor of *Gulf Coast* for three years. She currently teaches creative writing at Rice University as the Parks Fellow.

Lowell Mick White's work has been published in three dozen or so journals, most recently in *Callaloo, Iron Horse Literary Review*, and *Short Story*. In 1998 he was awarded the Dobie-Paisano Fellowship by the

University of Texas at Austin and the Texas Institute of Letters. He is currently a PhD student at Texas A&M University in College Station, where he specializes in creative writing, teaches prose fiction and freshman composition, and co-edits the journal *Big Tex[t]*.

Scott Wiggerman has published one book of poetry, *Vegetables and Other Relationships* (Plain View Press, 2000) and been published in *Borderlands: Texas Poetry Review, Windhover, Midwest Poetry Review, Spillway, Poesia, Paterson Literary Review* and others. Most recently, he has been published in the anthology *In the Arms of Words: Poems for Disaster Relief* (Sherman Asher, 2006). In addition, he is one of the two "cats" (i.e., editors) of Dos Gatos Press, which publishes the *Texas Poetry Calendar*, now in its tenth year. He lives in Austin.

Susan Wood is the author of three books of poetry, most recently *Asunder*, a National Poetry Series selection (Penguin 2001). A former Guggenheim fellow, she is the Gladys Louise Fox Professor of English at Rice University.

> "Gratification" appeared in *Five Points*, and was included in *The Best American Poetry 2006*, Guest Editor Billy Collins, Series Editor David Lehmann, published by Scribner Poetry. "In America" appeared in *The Virginia Quarterly Review;* "The Soul Bone" appeared in *Five Points*.

Adam Zagajewski was born in Lvov, Poland, and lives in Krakow and Chicago, where he teaches at the University of Chicago. He taught in the Creative Writing Program at the University of Houston for 19 years. He was awarded the 2004 Neustadt International Prize for Literature, and is the author of *Eternal Enemies, A Defense of Ardor* and *Without End: New and Selected Poems* (Farrar, Straus and Giroux). He is also the editor of *Polish Writers on Writing* (Trinity University Press),

> "Dolphins" appeared in *The New Republic*.

Mutabilis Press is a non-profit literary press dedicated to the publication of poetry, with focus on writers living or working in Houston and the surrounding area.

◆ ◆ ◆

For more information, see **www.mutabilispress.org**